Extinguishing Anxiety:

Whole Brain Strategies to Relieve Fear and Stress

Catherine M. Pittman, Ph.D., HSPP

Elizabeth M. Karle, MLIS

Foliadeux Press, LLC
South Bend, Indiana

Copyright © 2009 Catherine M. Pittman and Elizabeth M. Karle.

All rights reserved. Published in the United States of America by Foliadeux Press, LLC, South Bend, IN.

For ordering information contact:
www.extinguishinganxiety.com

Pittman, Catherine M.
    Extinguishing anxiety : whole brain strategies to relieve fear and stress / by Catherine M. Pittman and Elizabeth M. Karle.
        p. cm.
    Includes bibliographical references and index
    ISBN-13: 978-0-615-30904-0 (pbk.)
    1.   Anxiety – Treatment. 2. Behavior therapy.
    3.   Cognitive therapy. I. Karle, Elizabeth M. II. Title.

BF 575 .A6 P58
152.4

10 9 8 7 6 5 4 3 2 1

This book is dedicated to all of the animals that researchers have studied to provide us with our current understanding of the creation and extinction of fear and anxiety in the brain. Thanks to the contributions made by these rats, mice, dogs, primates (including humans), and others, our ability to cope with anxiety is greatly enhanced.

Acknowledgements

We gratefully acknowledge the many individuals who have contributed to this book in one way or another. The laboratory experiences provided by Sanford Dean, which were influenced by the theories of Wallace and Dorothy McAllister, started Catherine down the path of understanding the basis of fear conditioning. As a practicing psychologist, Catherine also owes a great debt to those who shared their struggles with anxiety, and trusted her with their treatment. By observing the courage shown by these individuals as they coped with anxiety disorders, Catherine acquired a great deal of knowledge about what approaches are useful; she will always appreciate those from whom she learned.

We wish to recognize the unfailing encouragement and the honest feedback provided by Clinical Neuropsychologist William Youngs, not only during the creation of this book, but also during many years of advising Catherine in her psychotherapy practice. Bill's professional experience, critical eye, and good humor make him a valued colleague.

Likewise, we are grateful for the careful and patient efforts of those who diligently read and edited this manuscript, including Arlene Forney, Sara Gardner, and Elaine Szarmach.

We also thank our families for their support of us during this process. Catherine's daughters, Arrianna and Melinda, were accepting of the countless hours their mother was in the library, and tolerant of many daily conversations focused on anxiety.

Elizabeth is extremely grateful for the support provided by her family, friends, and co-workers in her effort to overcome panic disorder and agoraphobia. Their role in the production of this book cannot be underestimated.

Contents

Chapter 1
About this Book

Do you need this book?

If you regularly struggle with anxiety or have been diagnosed with an anxiety disorder, you are facing a complex and challenging phenomenon. Anxiety is a multifaceted experience, affecting not only your emotions, but your thoughts, your behaviors, and your physical health. For most people, every day is complicated by some form of stress or anxiety. Some people only experience anxiety occasionally, but they find it limiting when it does occur. Other people find that worries fill their daily lives with discomfort. Whatever your specific experience of anxiety, this book will assist you in finding relief. Strategies to help you overcome anxiety are plentiful. We will show you how to make use of a variety of treatment methods that have been scientifically proven to be the most effective.

This book is designed to provide you with specific approaches that will actually *change your brain*. For this reason, a therapist may recommend this book to assist you. You will find relief and not be controlled by your anxiety if you are willing to learn how anxiety is created by your brain and how to use your whole brain to cope. Understanding the true nature of anxiety and setting meaningful, reasonable goals for yourself will be essential; this book will assist you in this two-step process. Our "whole brain" approach gives you specific strategies to use in order to cope with anxiety so that you can lead a more satisfying, even joyous, life.

What's New about Anxiety?

In the last decade, compelling new research has focused on the causes and treatment of anxiety. New technologies such as MRI, fMRI, and PET scans provide detailed information about the brain, and reveal the live brain in action, as we could never see it before.

Scientists now have a much more sophisticated understanding of how fear and anxiety develop. Perhaps even more significantly, they are discovering how the brain learns to *overcome* anxiety. New evidence suggests why anxiety affects some people in certain ways and not others. All of this is good news for those who suffer from anxiety, including those with disorders such as post-traumatic stress disorder, phobias, obsessive compulsive disorder, panic disorder, agoraphobia, and social anxiety disorder. No matter what the specific diagnosis, the underlying brain processes that lead to anxiety-related problems are similar, and operate in a relatively consistent manner.

As the basis for this book, we reviewed the currently evolving research on the neurophysiology of anxiety, as well as research on the most effective treatments. We integrated this information and filtered it through our own experiences to select what is most pragmatic and meaningful for those coping with anxiety on a daily basis. We think you will be as excited as we were when we recognized that in the past decade, many of the processes in the brain that create anxiety have been identified.

Because we now have a better understanding of how different parts of the brain acquire and maintain anxiety, we can make specific recommendations about how to approach treatment. In the past, treatments primarily focused on suppressing anxiety. We are learning, however, that it is more effective to train the brain to *resist* anxiety.

New evidence offers brain-based reasons why certain treatment methods work, and others are likely to fail. In addition, research shows why some of the oldest treatments for anxiety are still the best - while several of the most popular approaches (including some medications) are less than ideal given certain limitations in the brain's circuitry. We also recognize that different treatments are needed for different dimensions of anxiety; for example, an approach that helps to prevent anxiety provides little assistance in the midst of a panic attack.

We reviewed research from hundreds of studies and distilled what we learned into clear explanations, presented in brief, manageable sections. Each section is designed to help the reader comprehend specific points that are important in an overall understanding of anxiety. Therapists often find our descriptions and illustrations useful in explaining to their clients the nature of anxiety and the effects of certain treatments.

Our goal is to describe what is happening behind-the-scenes in the brain and what really works to change the brain's circuitry. We show you steps to take to actually "rewire" your brain to create a lasting change.

What Will You Learn?

The two key components to address in order to transform the anxious brain are *the brain's circuitry* and *the individual's thoughts and beliefs*. Cognitive behavioral therapy, considered by researchers around the world to be an effective form of treatment for anxiety,[1] focuses on both of these areas. Brain-imaging research shows that cognitive behavioral therapy results in changes in the brain in the areas involved in regulating fear and anxiety responses.[2] Cognitive behavioral techniques are incorporated into our "whole brain" approach. We want you to understand how and why these techniques are most effective against anxiety.

In order to change your anxious brain, you need to realize that there are emotional centers in your brain, as well as thought centers. And just as these distinct parts of the brain contribute to fear and worry, they also offer us a means to reduce anxiety. For example, you will become familiar with the **amygdala**, an emotional center that plays a large role in creating fear and anxiety. Using techniques that focus on the amygdala, you will discover how to design effective approaches to *bypass* or alter your brain's fight or flight circuitry. We will explain how fear is learned and how to overcome it through a process called **extinction**.

Perhaps most importantly, you will discover the power of **exposure-based therapy**. Just as physical therapy promotes healing in an injured body, exposure therapy promotes learning in the brain. Study after study shows that exposure therapy is effective.[3] We explain how you and your therapist can use it to "rehabilitate" or "re-wire" the specific parts of your brain that are creating anxiety. We also discuss how the thought centers in the brain, including the cortex, can be used to modify your brain's thinking processes to enable you to resist anxiety and minimize its effects.

In later chapters, we present the most recent information on the effects of various medications used to treat anxiety, and identify the strengths and limitations of each type. We examine how these medications might impact the course of treatment by focusing on how they affect brain processes - and considering that they have been studied primarily with short-term results in mind. With your doctor's guidance, this knowledge will help you to use medications in the most strategic and beneficial way: as one aspect of your overall treatment program.

By approaching anxiety and treatment from a variety of perspectives, we will show you how to use your whole brain to most effectively reduce your anxiety.

Why Will this Approach Work?

Why do we believe that our approach to managing anxiety will improve your quality of life? Our philosophy is that once the mystery of how something works is revealed, its power over you is reduced. We also trust that if you understand how various strategies impact the processes creating anxiety in your brain, including why they work, you will be more motivated to do what it takes to master your anxiety. You will be empowered by your knowledge, and no longer be a slave to your emotional reactions.

Already, numerous individuals have used the strategies in this book to improve their lives. For example, one man overcame his fear of crowds and resumed attending church services after years of avoidance. A woman with a history of poor attendance at work due to her fear of driving saw her absenteeism steadily decrease. Another woman recognized her arguments with her husband stemmed from her anxiety about attending family functions, and greatly improved her marriage by combating her anxiety, rather than her husband.

The organization of this book is designed to present information clearly, in compact portions that you can readily use. Occasionally, you will be asked to pause and *"Consider This"* in order to allow you to relate what you are learning to your own experiences. Please recognize that all of the chapters convey important information that is essential to learning how to manage anxiety. Trust us when we encourage you to read each section thoroughly to get the whole brain picture.

In some sections, we use scientific terminology to describe brain structures and processes so that you can use this book as a reliable reference tool. Note that we strive to give explanations and examples that make the complicated experience of anxiety easier to understand. It is our hope that by clearly explaining the latest theories and research on the causes and treatment of anxiety, we provide you with useful, cutting-edge information. This knowledge is very powerful.

Recognize that the more knowledge you have about your anxiety, the more power you have to defeat it. Not everyone will understand you or fully comprehend the anxiety you suffer. Your life will improve immeasurably, however, if YOU understand your anxiety on a neuropsychological level and take steps to gain control. Our whole brain approach will help you to manage your anxiety more successfully, and to live a happier, more productive life.

Chapter 2
Understanding What Causes Anxiety

The Brain Creates Anxiety

The human brain produces all of our sensations, perceptions, and experiences, including our emotions. While the achievements of cultures all over the world provide evidence of the amazing capabilities of the human brain, our brains also work within certain limits. For example, our sense organs determine what information is received by our brain. As a result, we do not perceive as many colors as bees do, but we can see more colors than dogs do. Based on the information received through our senses, as well as on stored memories, our brain processes, assembles and produces all of our experiences.

Every sunset we see, every pang of guilt we feel, every haunting memory of a lost love is, at one level, the result of certain processes in our brain. *How does our brain create the specific experience of anxiety?* Answering this question is an important objective of this book, since knowing how anxiety is created will help us to better understand how to combat it.

Anxiety sufferers are fortunate that the underlying neurological processes that give rise to anxiety and fear are better understood than those processes underlying other emotions. For this, we owe a debt of gratitude to a variety of devoted investigators,[1] and especially to the rats, pigeons, mice, dogs, and primates (including humans), that they have studied. That is why we dedicated this book to those unsung heroes, animals of all kinds, who have been studied to provide us with information about anxiety in the brain. Hundreds of studies have provided us with a wealth of information about the brain circuitry involved in fear, and the knowledge acquired from fear research is invaluable for those of us coping with anxiety.

Fear and anxiety are similar in that they arise from similar brain processes, and cause similar physiological and behavioral reactions. They both result from portions of our brain designed to help us deal with danger. They differ, however, in that **fear** is typically associated with a clear, present, and identifiable threat, whereas **anxiety** occurs in the absence of immediate peril. In other words, we feel fear when we actually are in trouble – like when the truck crosses the center line and heads toward us. We feel anxiety when we think about what might happen, but we are not, at the moment, in danger. An example of anxiety would be worrying that if you fly on a plane during your vacation, the plane may crash.

Although the emotions of fear and anxiety arise from similar processes in our brains, and feel similar in our bodies, fear is typically a stronger emotion, characterized by surges of arousal as well as the tendency to fight, flee, or freeze. Fear is about reacting to a threat. Anxiety is attempting to detect and prepare for a danger that may or may not materialize.

Studying other animals has taught us a great deal about the brain circuitry underlying anxiety. Because fear and anxiety arise from the portions of our brain designed to protect us from danger, those areas helped our ancestors survive and have been conserved through evolution in vertebrate species. When we examine the brains of other animals, particularly other mammals, we find that our brains share some of the same neural pathways and structures. These parts of our brains work in very similar ways from species to species. In fact, the emotional centers in our human brains are fundamentally equivalent to similar structures in other animals' brains.[2] Below are examples of a human brain (top) and a rat brain (bottom).

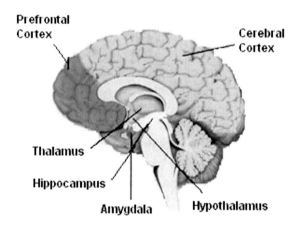

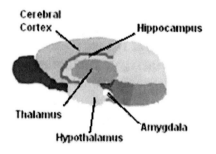

Primarily because of our larger cerebral cortexes, humans possess "higher" structures in our brains that give rise to what many consider to be uniquely human abilities (like language, logic, and consciousness). Unfortunately, these "higher" brain structures often take a back seat to the brain's emotional centers that cause fear and anxiety. Actually, our brain is wired in a way that allows our thought centers to be "overridden" by the emotion-producing portions of our brain. The emotional centers of the brain can "highjack" the rest of the brain and take charge. So, if you sometimes believe that all of your "superior" intelligence and self-knowledge does not do you much good when it comes to coping with anxiety, this is unfortunately a very accurate perception.

Typically, we are not consciously aware of what is going on in the emotion-producing centers in our brains; still, we feel their effects. The truth is, even though we are aware of many of our thoughts and emotions, the majority of the human brain operates without our conscious awareness. We don't have to think about most of the processes being accomplished by our brains, such as breathing, processing sounds, forming memories, and even reading this page.

As you read, for example, you are "unconscious" of the brain processes that make such reading possible. Reading is actually a very complicated task. If you refer to the "*Consider This*" segment below, you will find a summary of the visual processing that occurs without your awareness while reading. Thank goodness that we do not have to be thinking about these brain processes for them to operate.

Consider This:

What processes in your brain allow you to read this page?

As you read, photoreceptors in the back of your eyeball are responding to the light wavelengths reflected from the page. Photoreceptors encode features of the light into thousands of electrical charges that represent small, separate portions of your visual field. These individual electrical charges flow into the optic nerve, separated into two sets of electrical signals representing the left and right visual fields. Signals from your left visual field (some from your right eye and some from your left eye) travel to the right side of the back of your brain, and signals from your right visual field (some from each eye) travel to the left side of the back of your brain. The signals are processed in the primary and secondary visual association cortex in the back of your brain, resulting in a seamless perception of a whole page of text. Different portions of your visual field were processed in separate locations of your brain and "reassembled" into a unified image—this page of text.

So, while we tend to consider ourselves aware of what is happening in our heads, the truth is that much of the functioning of the brain is "back stage". Like a spectator watching a play, we generally are unaware of the activities going on behind the scenes (i.e., modifying the set, the lighting, and the music, not to mention directing and costuming the actors). Still, this is a big part of the overall production.

Consider This:

Can you think of other brain processes that occur without your awareness?

Some examples are:

Regulating a variety of processes including breathing, heart rate, digestion, body temperature, and hormonal levels

Seamlessly integrating many movements and sensations into complex behaviors that occur automatically, like typing or driving

Maintaining your balance and posture

Processing a variety of sounds, and the interpreted perceptions, such as knowing the location and nature of sounds heard

Automatically searching through millions of memories to recall a specific past experience

It is safe to say that in general, we are NOT aware of the brain processes giving rise to our sensations, thoughts, memories, and emotions. For this reason, we are dependent upon both animal and human research to uncover the nature of the brain circuitry that facilitates these unconscious processes. Such research involves laboratory testing, as well as monitoring simulated and real-life experiences with fear and anxiety.

A number of new technologies are helping us to watch the brain "in action" as we could never see it before. In many ways, the brain has become a new frontier.   Magnetic Resonance Imaging (MRI) takes high resolution three-dimensional pictures of the entire brain or of certain areas within the brain.   It is far superior to an x-ray.   Positron Emission Tomography Scans (PET) produce color-coded images that reveal fluctuating levels of substances such as oxygen or glucose being utilized in areas of the brain; this helps track what the brain is doing.   Functional MRI (fMRI) creates pictures of the brain at work by generating images reflecting changes in blood flow.

The knowledge obtained by studying the working brain assists researchers in recognizing patterns and tendencies in the creation and maintenance of anxiety. By summarizing and highlighting the most relevant research, this book will provide you with the capacity to understand and have more control over your own anxiety responses.

Is Anxiety Genetic?

An important issue to address before we begin discussing specific brain processes underlying anxiety is the role of genetics. People who suffer from chronic anxiety disorders understandably would like to know *why* they have difficulties with anxiety. They often ask whether they have genetically inherited anxiety problems. Rightly or wrongly, this question is a crucial one for several reasons. First, if a difficulty is identified as genetic, it is often seen by others (e.g., family, friends, employers) as a "real" problem which should be given medical attention or accommodation. Second, genetic disorders are often identified as something that an individual "can't help," so there is less stigma and embarrassment associated with having the disorder (e.g. it is not due to some weakness in character or unwillingness to fix the problem). Third, if the disorder is genetic, certain conclusions might be made about the usefulness of proposed treatment. So, identifying problems with anxiety as "genetic" can have repercussions that may affect how an individual is viewed by him/herself and others, as well as what treatment options are available.

Consider This:

Do your parents or other members of your family have difficulties with anxiety? (Consider worry, compulsions, panic, and general fearfulness as well as anxiety.) If so, are their difficulties similar to the ones you experience?

As you will learn, simplistic thinking about the causes of anxiety is not helpful. The correct answer to the question "Is anxiety genetic or environmental?" is "Yes." Anxiety is both genetic *and* environmental. Research has shown that both genetics and the environment are recognized as being influential in most anxiety disorders. In fact, many common diseases, from diabetes to heart ailments, are commonly thought to result from the complex interplay between genetic and environmental influences.[3]

Genetic Influences

To discuss genetic influences on anxiety, we must consider genetic influences on the brain. As soon as we are conceived, genes influence the development and organization of our brains, the nature of the circuits within our brains, and, to some extent, the types of connections that are formed.

Genes build the human brain according to certain consistent structural patterns. However, the unique set of genes that each person inherits creates a brain that is unique to that individual. We do not yet fully understand all the differences in our brains that could lead one person to be more susceptible to anxiety than another, but it is clear that genetics do play a role.

Perhaps some essential structure, chemical, or chemical process is missing or malfunctioning in the brains of individuals prone to anxiety? In later sections, we will identify brain structures that influence anxiety, such as the amygdala and neurotransmitters. Recent studies based on PET scans have found that children with anxiety disorders have smaller amygdalas than other children,[4] and individuals with panic disorder may be missing a particular type of serotonin receptor.[5] These specific findings suggest that it soon may be possible to identify just what differences within our brains lead to differences in susceptibility to anxiety. It is likely that some of these brain differences are inherited ones.

Speaking of genetics, it seems there are certain things which humans and other primates have a tendency to fear. People seem to develop phobias to snakes, water, heights, spiders, and enclosed spaces very easily – much more easily than to guns, cars, or knives, even though these latter objects are at least as likely to be associated with some kind of danger.[6] It is thought that there was a selective advantage to avoiding or fearing objects that posed a threat to our ancestors early in our evolutionary history. Perhaps our descendents will one day come to naturally fear some of the more modern hazards?

Even though we are just beginning to identify what might cause differences in anxiety between people, it seems clear that some individuals are born with a brain that has a predisposition for panic attacks or other anxiety disorders, while others have brains that seem to be much less likely to experience anxiety-related problems. In other words, we are born with varying degrees of fearfulness. Through no fault of our own, those of us who struggle with anxiety problems seem to have been dealt a hand that makes it somewhat difficult for our brains to function free from fear. But luckily, this is not the end of the story.

Environmental Influences

As you will see, the influence of the environment can *never* be ruled out. Experiences that occur both before we are born, as well as throughout our lives, impact the development of our brains. The substances our mothers were exposed to, the sounds we heard in the uterus, the amount of visual stimulation we had as infants, the way we were cared for by our parents, whether we took piano lessons - these factors and others all have been shown to affect brain development. In the age-old argument about whether nature (what we inherit) is more influential than nurture (what we experience), it must be conceded that nurture - or experience - has an indisputable impact on the brain.

The structures and circuits in our brain are very

responsive to our experiences; indeed, they are *designed* to be responsive. The brain's structure and function are shaped by our experiences because the brain is changeable. We can adapt. We can learn. What many people don't realize is that genetics can be affected, too. ***Our experiences can actually modify the influence of our genetic makeup!*** This suggests that we are not trapped by our genes because we can alter their impact.

Consider the implication of this statement: *In response to environmental input, genes modify their influence on the brain.* The most recent research shows that it is no longer "nature *or* nurture," but "nature *and* nurture". What happens to us in our daily lives actually can affect the influence genetics has on the very structure of our brains.

One study provides a good illustration of how the combination of nature and nurture influences anxiety. It followed individuals who developed difficulties with anxiety after experiencing Hurricanes Katrina and Rita.[7] The researchers found that people who had the short form of a specific gene (which influenced levels of a certain chemical in the brain) were more likely to develop post-traumatic stress disorder (PTSD), but only if they had experienced traumatic hurricane-related events AND had little social support.

Individuals who had inherited short forms of the gene from *both* parents (short/short) were most likely to develop PTSD. Those who had only one short gene (long/short) were less likely to develop PTSD. Individuals who inherited the long form of the gene from each parent were very unlikely to develop either PTSD or depression after the hurricane.

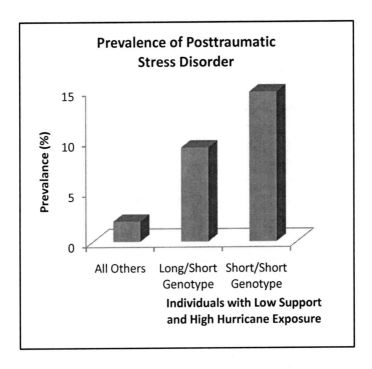

An important point to recognize is that this short gene did not cause anxiety or depression problems *unless* the person had been traumatized by the hurricane in the context of a lack of social support. Just having a traumatic hurricane experience or just lacking social support was not sufficient to result in PTSD. This shows that the gene has an effect only when it is "turned on" by specific experiences. This kind of evidence indicates that we should not assume genetics will dictate our brain's functioning. It *is* possible to change the impact of genetics, and the possibility of making changes despite our genetics gives us the hope we need to take control of our anxiety.

In her book, *Brave New Brain*, neuroscientist Nancy Andreasen encourages the reader to move away from thinking about "genetics *versus* environment:"

> Abandoning these false dichotomies gives a much better grasp on how life actually works, if we can handle the more complex way of thinking that arises when the world consists of continuities without arbitrary dividing boundaries. It is a more richly textured and colored world than the black-and-white dichotomies of mind versus brain or genes versus environment. It is also more true.[8]

Every day there are new examples of how the environment can impact genetic influences. Many genes have no impact until a certain experience propels them into action. Some genes will never be activated during a person's lifetime because the situation that activates them never occurs. Think of it in this way: even though the human brain has structures capable of understanding language, without the proper exposure to a specific language, a child will not learn to speak or understand it. We can speak English because we were taught it as children, but we've probably never been exposed to Russian. Thus, the language a child learns to understand is not based upon specific brain structures, but on the environment in which the child's brain develops.

The brain is designed to be very responsive to the environment. This responsiveness means that anxiety might be directly tied to environmental causes in some cases. For instance, child abuse has been found to result in changes in the brain that last into adulthood, and that make an individual more sensitive to stress later in life.[9]

A similar interaction can occur with regard to anxiety. Two daughters each may have inherited from their mother a genetic predisposition to have anxiety difficulties, for example, but only one daughter has life experiences that lead her predisposition to actually become an anxiety disorder. Once again, this illustrates the interactive relationship between genetics and the environment.

The experiences a person has clearly influence anxiety-based responding in other situations, as well. Often someone with no family history of anxiety disorders will develop a disorder as a result of experiencing distressing events. Even in brains that are less prone to anxiety, there are still some extremely traumatic situations, such as exposure to war or kidnapping, that seem capable of creating anxiety disorders in almost any brain, no matter what the genetic inheritance of the individual.

The Whole Picture

We now understand that our brain and its functioning result from a combination of genetic and non-genetic influences. Genetic factors can clearly increase the likelihood that a person has an anxious temperament. Non-genetic influences, such as the environment in which a child is raised, or the experience of traumatic events, are capable of modifying genetic influences. Conversely, genetic influences probably have an effect on the child's environment in some ways, too (e.g., parents may raise a child with an anxious temperament differently than one who is less anxious).

A number of scientists have put forth hypotheses as to how and why anxiety develops in some people but not in others. One of the leading researchers in this field is psychologist Susan Mineka of Northwestern University. Mineka and her colleague Richard Zinbarg note:

> Most of us might intuitively guess that anxiety disorders would typically develop during or following a frightening or traumatic event or during a period of significant stress when many of us experience some anxiety. Yet it is also obvious that not everyone undergoing traumas or highly stressful periods develops an anxiety disorder. Any good etiological theory must be able to account for this and many other apparent mysteries involved in who does and who does not develop an anxiety disorder.[10]

According to Mineka, differences in life experiences that occur before, during, and after a fear-evoking experience affect how much fear is acquired or maintained over time. Often, early experiences during childhood combine with temperamental vulnerabilities (e.g., being timid or shy) to make some individuals more or less susceptible to developing anxiety-related difficulties, depending upon contextual variables. The types of early experiences Mineka proposes as important include: early development of a sense of mastery or control over one's environment; becoming conditioned to fear certain situations or objects through watching others; and, verbal or cultural conditioning, where thoughts and ideas about what is safe and what is dangerous are communicated to the individual. [11] Some of this learning takes place as we observe our parents' behaviors and see what frightens or stresses them. Other times, our families, teachers or society blatantly tell us what to fear, such as strangers or germs.

Another influential researcher, psychologist David Barlow of Boston University, has spent decades designing effective treatment programs for anxiety. In Barlow's model, three factors contribute to the development of anxiety: genetics, diminished sense of control, and learning what is dangerous.[12] Barlow believes that contributions from numerous genes probably play a role in creating a general biological vulnerability to becoming anxious. This is the reason why traits such as nervousness, emotionality, or inhibition tend to run in families.

On top of this, failure to develop a sense of personal control over one's environment early on may predispose one to the development of chronic anxiety. More specifically, the parenting styles of our caregivers, especially if intrusive or overly protective, may limit our ability to explore our world, to try novel things, to develop new skills, or to cope with unexpected occurrences during childhood. According to Barlow, this limited opportunity to feel a sense of control or predictability seems to be at the root of a psychological vulnerability to anxiety. Later in life, this vulnerability also may serve to amplify stressful events for us.

Lastly, if an individual has learned, either through observation or through some other form of communication, to equate a specific object or event with danger, this can become a psychological vulnerability. In other words, a specific experience can convey a sense of threat or danger to a given situation. Consider how a child's awareness of his father's public-speaking anxiety, developed while watching his father pace nervously before giving a speech, may combine with other factors and ultimately lead that child to develop social anxiety.

As you can see, no one factor explains the development and maintenance of anxiety in everyone - a combination of genetic and environmental influences are typically involved. But just as we might learn through our experiences to be anxious, we can take steps to learn to be less anxious, too!

Because a combination of genetics and environment are involved in creating the experience of anxiety, it is likely that your difficulties with anxiety result from multiple, interacting causes. If you hadn't been born with your specific brain, you may not have been affected by anxiety. Or, if you hadn't been exposed to certain experiences, you might not be having these difficulties. The combination of your particular genetic background and the specific experiences you have had (or failed to have) during your life have shaped the way your brain operates now.

The good news is, despite the multiple influences on it, the brain is very malleable. It can learn and change. It should not be seen as doomed to operate in a rigid or fixed manner. Even genetic influences respond to environmental factors, including personal experience, viruses, diet, medications, and attitudes. As we will see, this is good news for anxiety sufferers!

<u>*Consider This*</u>:

Have you had specific experiences that have contributed to the development of your anxiety? What were they? How old were you at the time that these experiences occurred?

Some Philosophical Considerations

Let's reflect for a moment on an issue that sometimes troubles anxiety sufferers: whether or not their anxiety is their own fault. Taken another way, which person is more "responsible" for his or her anxiety difficulties: the person who inherits a disorder or one who acquires anxiety after a traumatic incident? The truth is, in each case, the individual has a lack of control over certain processes. Blaming that person for the problem by focusing on anxiety as a character flaw, or as a result of ineffective coping, doesn't seem beneficial. Therefore, it is best to acknowledge that the causes of anxiety are complex and multiple. Some processes are under an individual's control, others are not; no one really is to blame.

Just remember, you are the only person who needs to understand the whole picture. Whether others grasp it or not, your understanding of these processes will give you increased influence over the problem of anxiety. Our hope is that the information in this book will help you to clarify what you can change, as well as what is too difficult or impossible to modify, so that you may find a healthy balance between challenging and accepting your anxiety. We also will provide you with explanations of the methods you can use to make changes that will improve your life. So, let's get to it!

Chapter 3
How the Brain Creates Anxiety

Introducing the Amygdala

Recent research on both animals[1] and humans[2] suggests that the most important region of the brain with regard to experiencing and reacting to fear is the **amygdala**. We have an amygdala (uh-MIG-dull-uh) on each side of our brain. It is an almond-shaped structure composed of about a dozen different segments. Only a few of these segments are relevant to the experience of fear. The amygdala is made up of hundreds of circuits of cells dedicated to different purposes, including attachment, sexual behavior, anger, and aggression.

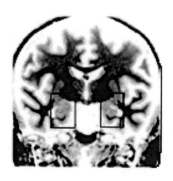

MRI scan (inverse image) with amygdala identified

The **lateral nucleus** of the amygdala is the portion of the brain that attaches emotional significance to situations or objects, just as other parts of the brain process the color or shape of objects. Our interest here is in the way the lateral nucleus attaches emotion (such as dread) to our experiences. Although the amygdala is involved in many of our positive emotional experiences, including happiness, love, and trust, in this book we will focus on the amygdala's role in creating fear and anxiety. We are not consciously aware of the process of the amygdala interpreting or attaching emotional significance, but the amygdala's emotional processing can have profound effects on our behavior.

All of the information that is received by the neurons in our sensory processing centers - information about what we are seeing or hearing, for example – is routed through the **thalamus** (THAL-uh-muss), a football-shaped relay center on top of the brain stem. Like a type of neural receptionist, the thalamus receives information from all kinds of sources, and directs this information to the appropriate brain centers for processing. Our amygdala receives information about our experiences from the thalamus through two different routes that researcher Joseph LeDoux[3] has dubbed the *low road* and the *high road*. Perhaps because of our familiarity with driving in the Chicago area, we tend to think of the two pathways as the *express lane* and the *local lane*. On the next page you can see a graphic representation of the express and local lanes.

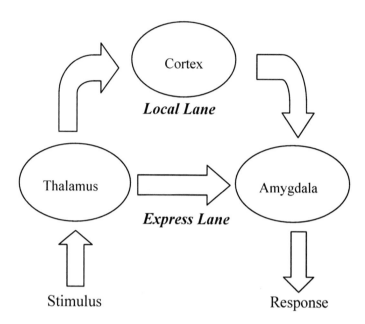

One way that information comes to the amygdala is directly from the thalamus. This is like an ***express lane***. Neural impulses travel this express route directly from the thalamus *before* the sensations are sent to other areas of the brain for further, more in-depth processing. Information from the thalamus is not very detailed, but it comes *very* quickly; that is why it is easy for us to think of this route as the "express lane".

The thalamus also sends this information on to the **sensory cortex**, where additional processing and refining of the information occurs. Then the sensory cortex sends *detailed* information to the amygdala. This longer route, from thalamus to sensory cortex to the amygdala, is more like taking the ***local lane.*** In our highway analogy, this route is the slower one that allows for more information to "merge" with the sensory information as it is being processed.

Express lane: thalamus → amygdala

Local lane: thalamus → sensory cortex → amygdala

The neural impulses being delivered from the sensory cortex to the amygdala via the local lanes provide information that is more complete and descriptive, but this information also takes longer to reach the amygdala. Think of the signals from the local lanes (through both the thalamus and sensory cortex) as having the sharp details and clear presentation characteristic of a high-resolution digital color photograph, while the signals coming from the express lane (directly from the thalamus) have the grainy, unfocused characteristics of a blurry black and white picture.

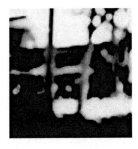
via express lane

via local lane

In the animal kingdom, one of the most important functions of the amygdala is to produce a rapid fear response. The amygdala's use of the vague, but more quickly available, "express" information from the thalamus has probably saved the lives of countless animals, including our ancestors. That is the reason this brain circuitry has been retained. For example, a sudden dark-colored movement in the bushes that is rapidly processed by the thalamus and sent directly to the amygdala in its crude form may result in an individual beginning to flee, only to halt a moment later as input from the more detail-oriented sensory cortex provides sufficient descriptive information to recognize the movement as the approach of a friendly dog.

Responding quickly is essential in many life-or-death situations, when a fraction of a second delay can have deadly costs. So it is not surprising that, through evolution, the brain has retained this pathway for the rapid routing of information. The impulses traveling the local route may take less than a second, but the messages traveling the express route are much faster, and must be measured in *milliseconds* (thousandths of a second)! After all, it is better to react defensively first, and risk an unnecessary escape, then to wait for more information and lose valuable time in the process.

A Quick Escape

The quick initiation of our escape mechanism is an essential function of the amygdala that depends on two portions of the amygdala, the lateral nucleus and the central nucleus. Each of these nuclei plays a specific role in the escape process.

Amygdala

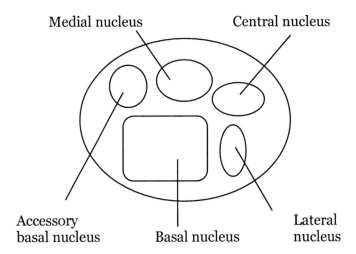

Medial nucleus   Central nucleus

Accessory
basal nucleus   Basal nucleus   Lateral
nucleus

On the basis of rapidly-provided but sometimes vague
sensations, such as hearing a sound or seeing a
movement, the **lateral nucleus** of the amygdala
assesses the emotional significance of an event. If the
lateral nucleus interprets the information as signaling
danger, it activates the central nucleus of the amygdala,
which initiates a fear-motivated behavioral response.
The **central nucleus** is the control center in the
amygdala that has the connections to rapidly produce
fear-related responses ranging from increased heart
rate and adrenalin rush, to becoming immobile or
motionless (freezing in place).

The lateral nucleus of the amygdala can also send
inhibitory messages to the central nucleus when
new information is provided. Inhibitory messages tell
the central nucleus to cancel or inhibit the escape
behavior. All of this communication between these
segments of the amygdala can occur *before* the sensory

information is completely processed by the parts of our cortex that provide us with awareness of the experience. We may not be aware of what we saw or reacted to for a second or so, because it takes some time for the brain to process the sensory information in areas of the cortex called **convergence zones**. In these convergence zones, the brain creates a more global and detailed perception - the perception we are aware of, that travels on the local lanes. After this level of processing is accomplished in our cortex, we consciously know something is going on.

As you can see, fear-related experiences are processed in different areas of the brain on different time schedules and with differing levels of conscious awareness. Your amygdala can initiate an escape response *before* other parts of your brain have even had time to process the information. In fact, in some cases, your amygdala can initiate and inhibit an escape response faster than you can recognize what it was that caused your reaction in the first place!

Consider the implications of this capacity of the brain. Our sensory systems can provide raw sensory information (sounds, images, smells) to the amygdala, which evaluates and responds to them before we are even consciously aware of what has occurred. How many times have you reacted quickly to avoid a dangerous situation - swerving around an oncoming car, for example - before you have had time to assess the situation or even to feel fear? This streamlined emotional processing and quick response has been essential for survival, but it also is not readily modified by our conscious efforts.

Consider This:

*Can you think of times that you reacted **before** you had time to think? Were you aware of the bodily sensations that accompanied the quick response?*

You now know that fear becomes associated with certain objects or situations, and that the amygdala can instantly initiate complex sets of responses without input from other areas of the brain. This knowledge provides you with an understanding of why it is difficult to modify our own fear and anxiety responses. But we CAN learn to modify these fear responses if we learn to speak the **"language of the amygdala."**

The Language of the Amygdala

If you want to communicate with the amygdala, you will need to use a language of **associations**, not one of cause and effect. This is very important to realize. For fear or anxiety to be *associated* with a certain object or situation, the object or situation need not actually be harmful or dangerous. For an association to develop, the object need only be *experienced at the same time* that some strongly arousing, typically fear-eliciting event is occurring.

We have known about this association-based learning process, called **Classical Conditioning**, for over a century - ever since Russian physiologist Ivan Pavlov discovered that dogs would salivate to the sound of a bell. What we are currently learning, based on recent research, is the neurological language of fear and anxiety. Developing an understanding of these neurological processes gives us clear suggestions about how to modify the associations through learning and/or medication. We are discovering how to speak the language of the amygdala.

The Importance of the Neurology of Fear

An example can help clarify what we know about the neurological processes involved in fear. Imagine a person being confronted by a dog. The sight, sound, and smell of the dog are processed by the thalamus and relayed directly to the lateral amygdala (via the express lane) as well as to the sensory cortex (via the local lane). The sensory information resulting from exposure to the dog is relayed to the lateral amygdala, but fear does not automatically result from receiving this information. *Only* if this sensory information is being processed in the lateral amygdala ***immediately before or at the same time as*** the occurrence of a very strong negative experience, such as a threatening or biting dog, will this sensory information in the amygdala change the neurons in the brain in such a way that *fear will be learned.*

This is how a change in the lateral amygdala would result in a learned fear of dogs: when a painful or strong experience such as a dog bite occurs at approximately the same time that nerve cells are relaying sensory information about the dog's appearance and other cues, the nerve cells conducting the sensory information elicit strong emotional excitation in the amygdala. The modification of these nerve cells occurs as a result of the **pairing** of the two experiences: one relatively neutral (the dog) and one which is strong or painful (the bite). We refer to the dog as neutral, because any particular dog could be friendly, excitable, dull, ambivalent, or mean.

It should be remembered that the two experiences (meeting the dog and being bitten) need NOT have a cause/effect relationship; *they need only occur together in time* (**temporal relationship**). This is why, after a person experiences an automobile accident, the honking of a horn can cause that person a tremendous amount of anxiety, even though the accident was not caused by the horn. ***The experiences occurred at the same time and became associated with one another.*** The amygdala is very sensitive to this type of association.

A Lesson in Classical Conditioning

After September 11th, 2001, millions of Americans reduced their use of air travel, and increased their use of long distance driving. Ironically, instead of keeping travelers safer, this avoidance of flying actually resulted in more fatalities. In fact, the number of Americans who died in automobile accidents by avoiding the risk of flying was greater than the number of passengers killed on the four fatal flights.[4] This is a clear example of how our fears may not have the protective value that they are intended to have.

The amygdalas of millions of Americans were clearly involved in the avoidance of flying. The increased fear of flying that occurred after September 11th was not solely a logical decision made after a terrorist attack. It was also based on a specific association that was experienced by millions of

Americans: repeatedly witnessing a plane flying into a building and exploding into flames. This association, which paired the image of a plane with a horrific outcome, created a connection between the image of a plane and disastrous consequences. The fact that air travel actually became safer after September 11th did not matter. In addition, this example illustrates that an individual can learn fear and anxiety by watching others; a negative incident does not necessarily have to happen directly to that individual.

Because of the experiences of millions of amygdalas across the country, airplanes became associated with fear. This association process is standard classical conditioning. Being able to identify the associations formed between events as a result of classical conditioning will help you to recognize daily events that trigger your anxiety. First, we need to identify two important terms: a **Trigger** and a **Negative Event**. In our September 11th example, the Trigger is the plane, and the death and destruction that was paired with the plane is (obviously) a Negative Event. The Trigger is originally a neutral object or event (not causing any fear or anxiety), but it comes to cause a fearful reaction as a result of the conditioning process. See Figure 3.1 for a visual depiction of this explanation.

Figure 3.1

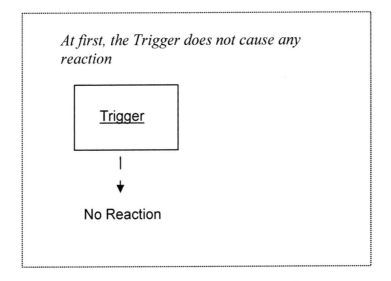

At first, the Trigger does not cause any reaction

The reason that we call this stimulus a Trigger is because this stimulus will come to trigger a reaction after **conditioning.** What is conditioning, and how does conditioning occur? Conditioning occurs when the Trigger gets paired with a Negative Event that automatically causes emotional responding.

Now, compare experiencing this neutral trigger with a more emotion-arousing Negative Event. Some events can be considered Negative Events because they automatically will result in discomfort, pain, or other negative responses. An example of a Negative Event could be an accident that causes an injury. In Figure 3.2, you can see that a Negative Event leads to a very different response than the Trigger does.

Figure 3.2

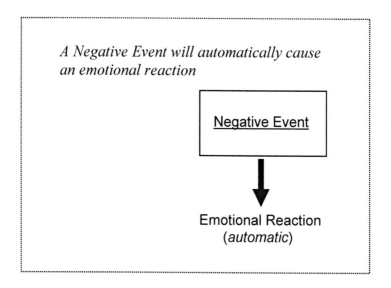

A Negative Event will automatically cause an emotional reaction

Negative Event

Emotional Reaction
(*automatic*)

If you look at Figure 3.3, you will see that now these two experiences have been paired together: a Negative Event has been paired with the Trigger. This negative event is something that causes some negative Emotional Reaction, usually distress or pain. In the diagram in Figure 3.3, the line connecting the two boxes signifies a pairing between the Trigger and the Negative Event. This reminds us that the Negative Event occurs shortly after the Trigger. The two are paired together, with the Negative Event following the Trigger in time.

In Figure 3.3, you also see the pairing has caused the Trigger to result in a Fear Reaction. This Fear Reaction is new; it did not occur before the pairing of the Trigger with the Negative Event.

Figure 3.3

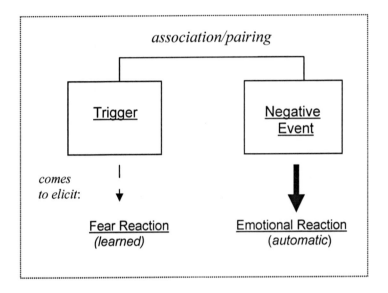

The Fear Reaction was established in the lateral amygdala, which learns on the basis of associations such as this. The pairing (or association) of the Trigger and the Negative Event has changed the emotional reaction to the Trigger. Before, the Trigger was neutral. Now, the Trigger will cause a Fear Reaction. The Fear Reaction is *learned* (conditioned) in the lateral amygdala. The lateral amygdala is the part of the brain that creates a neural connection between the Trigger and Fear.

Let's look at a real experience in which this may occur. In a car accident, for example, the honking horn is the Trigger and the <u>actual</u> accident is the Negative Event. Normally, a horn does not cause a strong emotional reaction. For a person to learn to fear the

Trigger (horn), it must be paired with a Negative Event (accident). See Figure 3.4 for an illustration of how this pairing occurs. The sound of the horn occurs just before the accident. Note that the horn does not *cause* the accident; it is just *associated* with the accident. The accident results in the person being injured and experiencing pain. You can see how the accident qualifies as what we have been calling a Negative Event, and that the horn is the Trigger that has been paired with this Negative Event.

The pairing of the Horn and the Accident results in a change in the lateral amygdala. Now, whenever the amygdala hears a Horn, it will produce a Fear Reaction.

Figure 3.4

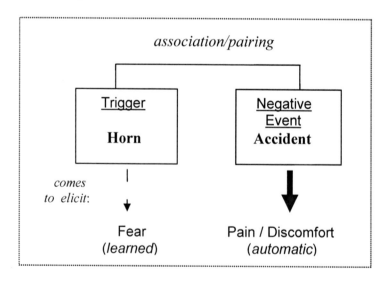

Ordinarily, the amygdala will learn to fear the horn if the horn precedes the accident in time, but not by much. The strongest conditioning occurs when the

Trigger occurs less than a second before the Negative Event. This is why, after an accident, the sight of an intersection, the sound of a horn, the smell of burned rubber, or even the sensation of braking, can cause a person to feel fear. After the accident, these Triggers are conditioned to produce fear because they were experienced just before the accident. As you can see, multiple triggers (intersection, horn, burned rubber, etc.) can be conditioned to cause fear in one traumatic experience. These triggers can be considered "cues" for fear or anxiety. *It is the Trigger being paired with the Negative Experience that makes the Trigger produce fear or anxiety.* The Trigger acquires the ability to elicit anxiety because the amygdala has detected that the trigger was experienced just prior to the negative experience.

The dotted line from the trigger to fear in Figure 3.4 indicates that the trigger comes to elicit fear or anxiety over time as a result of *learning* that occurs in the lateral amygdala. You should be able to remember the difference between the trigger and the negative event by noting the symbols that connect the stimuli and responses in the diagram. The bold arrow from the negative event to pain indicates that there is an *automatic* connection between the negative event (accident) and the negative response (pain). In most cases, the negative event will automatically produce a certain response. In contrast, the connection between the trigger and fear or anxiety is a connection that is *created* by the amygdala as a result of the pairing of the trigger (horn) and negative event (accident). We use the dotted line to signify that this is a "learned" association.

The amygdala connects the sensory information from the accident (the sights, sounds, smells) with the emotion of fear.   After the amygdala creates the connection between this sensory information and the emotional memory, we'll hear a horn and feel anxious.

Consider This:

> *As you experience a typical day, look for situations in which you can practice developing an awareness of the language of the amygdala. Look for certain stimuli (sights, sounds, smells) that get paired with negative experiences. These types of pairings are the focus of the watchful amygdala, so try to become aware of them.*

> *Learn to identify triggers in negative situations, because they have the potential to elicit anxiety.*

Before you get the idea that you might be better off without your amygdala, remember that classical conditioning produces associations for positive emotions, too. For example, if your special someone gives you a necklace as a gift, you will probably feel warmth and love for your mate. Later, when you see the necklace in the mirror, the association formed between the necklace and the emotion of love will make you feel happiness again. Had this necklace not been paired with the affectionate feelings you have for your significant other, it would simply be just another piece of jewelry. So the amygdala helps us feel positive emotions also, and we wouldn't want to get rid of it completely!

Learning to Diagram in the Language of the Amygdala

Learning to identify triggers and the negative events they have been associated with is very helpful in understanding the language of the amygdala and its role in producing anxiety. Here are some helpful guidelines. Both the trigger and the negative event are **stimuli**, meaning that they are objects or events that you see, hear, feel, or experience. The trigger differs from the negative event because you *learn* to fear or be anxious about the trigger, whereas the negative event is something that you don't have to learn to react to. The trigger is something that you often want to stop responding to, but which activates emotions in you, even if you know the emotions are not logical. Often these emotions are ones that other people are *not* feeling because they have not had the same conditioning experience that your amygdala has had.

The negative event is something that caused an unpleasant emotional response in you. It could have been a dog bite, a panic attack, or an argument with someone. The fact that the trigger was paired with the negative event made the trigger activate your fear or anxiety. Usually the negative event comes right after the trigger, like a dog bite coming after a growling dog, a panic attack happening after you get on a bus, or an argument occurring after you ride in the elevator with your boss.

So, when you are reacting to a dog, a bus or an elevator, and others are saying "There is no reason to be so anxious!" you can say "Try to tell that to my amygdala!" The reason that you are reacting to this trigger is because the trigger has been paired with a negative experience. This pairing is what leads the amygdala to create an emotional response to the trigger.

<u>Consider This</u>:

In most cases, the Trigger and Negative Experience boxes will be the only parts of the diagram that you need to figure out. Use this all-purpose diagram as a guideline for understanding the language of the amygdala. Fill in the ???

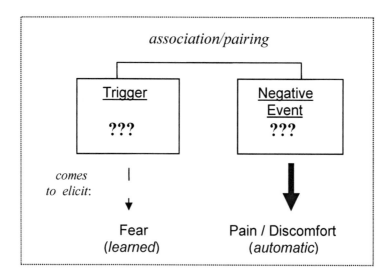

The question to answer: "What <u>Trigger</u> was paired with what <u>Negative Event</u>?"

Fear learning can occur to a variety of objects, sounds, or situations, as long as they are associated in time with a strong negative event. A Vietnam veteran who thought he had recovered from his traumatic war experiences suddenly began feeling panicky in the mornings again. When he examined his morning routine, he realized he was having a strong fear response in reaction to the scent of a particular type of soap. When he showered and smelled the fragrance of that soap, he became anxious. He did not immediately understand why he was feeling so anxious when he showered, until he remembered that he had used that same soap during the war.

In the language of the amygdala, the smell of this soap (trigger) had become associated with the traumatic events of combat, including injuries and feelings of terror (negative experience) as in Figure 3.5.

Figure 3.5

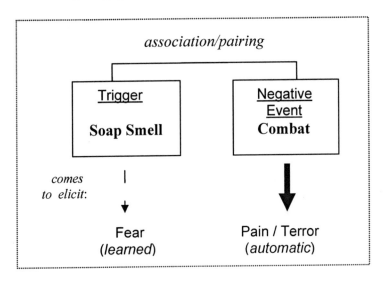

Take some time to learn to use the diagram with the arrows, boxes and responses, because it is the **language of the amygdala.** Knowing this language gives you increased capacity to communicate with the amygdala. You need to understand how nerve cells in the amygdala are programmed on the basis of **association** - the occurrence of two events one after the other - and remember that a cause/effect relationship is not necessary. This language of the amygdala is a powerful one. It is important for you to remember just how potent and lasting fear associations created by the amygdala can be.

Consider This:

See if you can draw diagrams to identify examples of pairings that a person may experience which could cause fear responses. Consider a mother who yells at and then spanks her child. Can you identify the **trigger** *and* **negative event** *that lead to fear and to pain/discomfort? What about a woman who is sexually assaulted by a red-haired man with a British accent? What are the triggers in this situation, which may later cause anxiety in this woman's life? You can see the correct diagrams in Appendix A.*

Conditioned Fear Can Lead to More Fear

Once an event or object has become a trigger for fear or anxiety, whatever gets paired with it becomes capable of causing anxiety in the language of the amygdala. This process is known as **higher order conditioning**. This means that once a trigger is causing a fear response, it can begin to act like a negative event itself, and whatever is paired with it can elicit a similar, but weaker, emotional reaction. See Figure 3.6. As an example, after being paired with a spanking, a parent's yelling can come to elicit fear. Yelling has become a trigger. Then, another trigger (trigger $_2$) can be paired with the original trigger, and will come to elicit a similar, although somewhat weaker, emotional response. So if a parent tends to call you by your full name (including your middle name) just before yelling at you, your middle name will come to elicit a negative emotional reaction, such as apprehension.

Figure 3.6

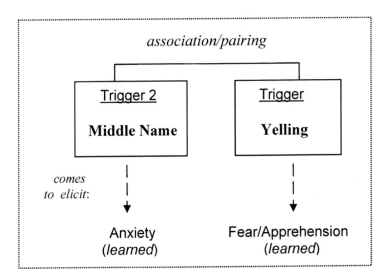

The amygdala is exquisitely aware of the pairing of events which are associated with fear or danger. It can create connections in your brain that cause you to react with anxiety to any cues that it interprets as predicting danger. This means that, as in Figure 3.6, sometimes the trigger is paired with another trigger, rather than a negative event. The amygdala can build on already established fears to create new ones.

Life With and Without the Amygdala

Only recently have we begun to learn the neurological language of the amygdala and been able to determine how the cells in the amygdala learn and store emotional information. Because memories created by the lateral amygdala about emotional experiences are not stored in a way that is consciously accessible to us, we are often completely unaware of the process of learning fear. In fact, the *emotional* memories formed by the amygdala are completely separate from the types of memories formed by other parts of our brain. This becomes most apparent when we examine the behavior of people who have impaired amygdalas, as a result of brain damage (like a stroke or a gunshot wound) or after neurosurgery performed to control seizures.

Individuals without properly functioning amygdalas are able to report clear memories of events occurring one after another—like a loud, blinking light followed by a startling noise. But, without an amygdala, they do not acquire the emotional memory about the blinking light that those of us with an intact amygdala would acquire.[5] An Iraqi War veteran without an amygdala would not acquire a fear response to the sound of a helicopter, even if that sound were followed by a traumatic injury, yet the veteran may remember the sequence of traumatic events in battle very clearly.

The reverse is also true: a person who has a functioning amygdala but an impaired memory for events can form *emotional* memories, even when memories for past events are impaired or absent. For example, a woman who had severe Korsakoff's syndrome, a memory disorder often associated with chronic alcoholism, could not identify her doctor or hospital, despite the fact that she had been an inpatient for five years.[6] She did not know the name of the nurse who had cared for her for at least six months, and could not remember details of a story told to her after only three minutes.

At the same time, however, this woman's amygdala demonstrated the ability to create *emotional* memories. When a physician reached out and stuck her hand with a pin hidden between his fingers, she apparently formed an *emotional* memory (fear) of this incident. The next day, when he visited her and reached toward her hand again, she quickly withdrew her hand, even though she had no specific memory of him harming her. In fact, she was not able to remember ever seeing him before! She had no *conscious* knowledge of why she withdrew her hand. Nevertheless, her amygdala was operating, and had created an *emotional* memory, identifying this man's hand reaching toward her as a signal of danger, even if other types of memories had not been preserved.

Consider This:

Have you ever had an emotional memory that you couldn't explain related to someone you knew? Someone whose appearance or mannerisms troubled you, but you were unaware of the reason? Do you think your amygdala was involved in this memory?

As you are no doubt beginning to recognize, even though the memories it creates are not conscious, the amygdala is key in creating our fears and anxieties. In the next chapter, we will examine how the amygdala creates anxiety in our bodies. You will see that the amygdala has a great deal of influence over our physical reactions to anxiety-provoking situations.

Chapter 4
Fear and Anxiety in the Body

The Freeze/Fight/Flight Response

You are no doubt familiar with the concept of the "fight or flight" response. All vertebrate animals have programmed "emergency response" routines that have served our species well for hundreds of thousands of years. When we are in danger, specific circuitry in our brains springs into action, and a variety of physiological processes occur in our bodies without our control or awareness. Although this emergency routine is commonly referred to as the "fight or flight" response, Joseph LeDoux, author of *The Emotional Brain*,[1] makes a good argument that the response should be called the Freeze/Fight/Flight response, because "freezing" often comes first. Whether we study animals in the laboratory or humans under traumatic conditions, we often observe the tendency to remain motionless or to feel too overtaken with fear to respond. Perhaps you too have experienced not only the desire to flee or fight, but also a feeling of temporary immobility when you are extremely anxious.

Walter Cannon first recognized the pattern of responding called "flight or fight" in 1929, but it was Hans Selye in the 1930s who recognized that, not only the human body, but the bodies of other animals have a surprisingly similar reaction to a broad set of stressors.[2] Usually our bodies respond in a way that is specific to the situation, as when our pupils contract in bright light but dilate when it is dark, or when we shiver in the cold but sweat in hot temperatures. What Selye discovered is that the rats that he was studying had similar bodily responses even when the situations they encountered were very different. A variety of stressful situations—being given repeated injections, being accidentally dropped on the floor, being chased with a broom (Selye was a rather clumsy experimenter in his early days!) - all of these events seemed to create the same set of physiological reactions in the rats. Selye had put his finger on a programmed set of responses that animals use when they are under what he called "**stress**," a term he borrowed from engineering.

Selye had discovered a response characteristic of many animals (including birds, reptiles, and rats as well as humans). We all have an eerily similar programmed set of physiological responses that allow us to respond quickly in a dangerous situation. We humans often like to think of ourselves as superior, but in terms of these programmed responses, we operate in much the same manner as other vertebrate species. Whether we are being chased by a bear, asked to dance at a party, or being told we are fired, our bodies react in a surprisingly similar way to the bodies of those rats being chased with a broom.

The set of responses known as the **stress response** includes increased heart rate and blood pressure, rapid breathing, dilated pupils, a sudden availability of blood flow in the extremities, increased perspiration, and slowed digestion. They result from the activation of the sympathetic nervous system and the influence of adrenaline.

These physiological changes are very useful in preparing an animal to escape from danger, and many of our ancestors were probably saved by swift and automatic responses that allowed them to escape the jaws of a predator or the pursuit of an enemy.

Freeze/Fight/Flight in the Twenty First Century

Unfortunately, the stress response is not always useful in responding to the threats that we humans face today. An increased heart rate, perspiration, and preparation in your extremities to run or fight may help you to escape from a bear, but they are not particularly useful when your boss tells you to increase productivity or face termination, when you receive an overdue notice on your mortgage payment, or when your teenage daughter starts arguing with you. Yet these physiological responses are hard-wired into you, and you have little control of the brain processes that put them into action.

Consider This:

Can you think of a time that your stress response kicked into action when it was not helpful at all? In other words, did you ever experience increased heart rate and perspiration and feel a surge of energy when it was counterproductive to have these responses? At times, these programmed responses actually interfere with what you are trying to accomplish.

Learning how the stress response operates in our bodies reminds us that even though we consider ourselves to be in control (or at least conscious) of what goes on inside ourselves, many of our physiological and behavioral responses are automatic, not governed by our higher level thinking processes. As we discussed in Chapter 2, a lack of awareness and control of many processes is characteristic of the majority of brain processing. You are not aware of how your brain translates vibrations in the air into electrical charges in neurons that it can interpret as a Bruce Springsteen song, and you are not aware of the signals being sent to your muscles to maintain an upright posture, are you?

In a similar way, you are not in control, or even aware, of many of the brain processes that underlie the stress response. The stress response is a set of brain processes and resulting physiological and behavioral changes that have been part of vertebrate responding for hundreds of thousands of years, and in order to operate quickly and automatically enough to be effective, it *cannot* be based on the "higher" (cortex-based) thinking processes that we humans are so proud of possessing. It probably will not surprise you that the circuits that put the stress response into action are - where else? In the amygdala.

<u>Consider This</u>:

Take a few deep, slow breaths. Inhale slowly and deeply, and exhale fully. Do not force your breathing. Breathe gently both in and out. Don't worry about whether or not you are breathing through your mouth or nose— just breathe in a comfortable manner. Note how the deliberate attempt to slow and deepen your breathing affects you. Does it have a calming effect for you?

Back to the Amygdala

Two important parts of the amygdala were mentioned in Chapter 3. The **lateral nucleus** is the portion of the amygdala that monitors information from various senses. It is watching for indications of danger. When the lateral nucleus of the amygdala receives information it identifies as threatening, it sends a message to the central nucleus which can initiate a complex set of physiological responses. The **central nucleus** is like an ignition switch that puts the stress response into action. It can be thought of as the starter button of the amygdala. Just as you are the one who controls the ignition in your car, the central nucleus is controlled by the lateral nucleus of the amygdala.

The central nucleus of the amygdala sends messages to a variety of other parts of the brain, and in fact, the amygdala should be thought of as a very well connected player in brain processes. The amygdala can influence a surprising number of processes through its many connections, including our attention to and interpretation of sensations, our consciousness, our memories, and our actions. The amygdala's connections allow it to influence and even circumvent many of the higher level processes in our brain. This capability of the amygdala to override other brain processes is why, when the lateral nucleus of the amygdala senses you are in danger and activates the central nucleus, you find your attention drawn to specific objects, have difficulty concentrating on or remembering other things, and perform behaviors without thinking beforehand. It is as if a wrench has been thrown into the works of your thinking processes. The central nucleus of the amygdala, through its many neural connections, simply overrides the higher level brain processes that, in a moment of danger, seem to be luxuries that must take a back seat to protecting your safety.

One of the most important parts of the brain that the amygdala is connected to is the **hypothalamus**, a peanut-sized region of the brain that controls a variety of bodily processes.

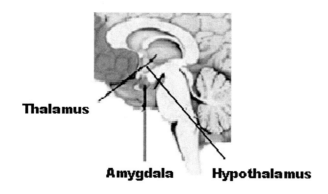

Thalamus

Amygdala   **Hypothalamus**

This connection to the hypothalamus allows the amygdala to have very widespread effects on your whole body's functioning. Because the central nucleus of the amygdala is connected to the hypothalamus, it can initiate the release of **adrenaline,** also called epinephrine.

The amygdala's signals also can activate the **sympathetic nervous system.** This process is responsible for the physiological changes we see in the body when the stress response occurs. It is an evolutionarily ancient response that happens in a fraction of a second, and it occurs without our conscious awareness or control. Your heart begins pounding, your palms sweat, and you feel primed for action, before you have time to think. You may not even know what set off the response for a moment or two. This is because the brain is organized in such a way that emotional processing related to fear in the amygdala occurs in milliseconds. Other types of processing, such as perception, thinking, and retrieving memories (in higher levels of the cerebral cortex), may take more than a second to occur.

Some Functions of the Sympathetic Nervous System:

accelerate heartbeat	slow digestion
increase respiration	dilate pupils
inhibit saliva production	raise blood pressure
increase perspiration	relax bladder

Remember that the amygdala is capable of identifying a situation as dangerous before the rest of the brain knows exactly what the situation is. Consider the advantages of having the dangerous/safe dimensions of an object or situation identified – courtesy of your amygdala – before other brain processing is completed. It could save your life! This is why this emergency response system has been preserved with little change through our evolution.

> *Consider This:*
>
> *When you feel startled by something, have you noticed how your amygdala can make your body react before you have time to think? Consider the physical responses you feel in your body after a startling event. How often do you recognize what startled you only after your body has reacted? Notice how different parts of your brain are reacting on different time lines.*

What about the Rest of My Brain?

The portion of your brain that is responsible for the initiation of fear, anxiety, and the stress response would fit in the palm of your hand. The amygdala, the hypothalamus, and the attached pituitary gland are essential in this process. But what about the rest of the human brain? What is the rest of the human brain doing when these ancient processes are occurring?

As humans, we pride ourselves on the crowning achievements of the human brain, with its capacity for reasoning, planning, language, and invention. It is somewhat shocking to learn that these capabilities, housed in the upper, tremendously wrinkled part of our brain known as the **cerebral cortex**, are so easily influenced by the smaller, older portion of the brain that is responsible for the stress response. But the amygdala has this kind of influence. In fact, our brains are wired not only to allow the amygdala to override some of the processes occurring in the cerebral cortex, but also to mute the input of the cerebral cortex in times of stress. At such times, we are wired to operate *without thinking.*

While the amygdala is solidly wired into many regions of the brain, and can have widespread effects, the connections do not go both ways. The neural connections from the higher levels of the cerebral cortex to the amygdala are surprisingly few. The portions of our cortex in which our perceptual, thinking, and speaking processes occur are only wired into one portion of the amygdala - the central nucleus, the ignition switch in the amygdala. The lateral nucleus, which is responsible for detecting, processing, and perceiving fear-related experiences, is not directly influenced by the highest levels of our brain because these are not even wired to provide input. Though this situation is frustrating, it is understandable in terms of brain evolution. Waiting for such input, which depends on processing that may take seconds to occur, is a luxury that cannot be risked in dangerous situations.

For researchers, however, there are some advantages of this state of affairs. Since the brain systems underlying fear are so similar in all animals, investigators have been able to study these processes more easily than many other emotional processes in the human brain. Because of many studies conducted on rats and mice, who share this emergency response system, our understanding of these processes has greatly increased. In the past several decades, research has provided new information on how to influence the processes that give rise to anxiety, and to give relief to those who suffer from it. This research has proved very helpful in knowing how to combat anxiety, and it is part of the basis of this book.

We want to acknowledge that it can be discouraging to know that your clearest thinking skills and personal insights are essentially disabled by the ancient brain structures that create your fear-related difficulties. It is frustrating to realize that all of your cortex-based thinking can be taken over by the amygdala. *Once you have this knowledge, however, it can be used to your advantage.* The key is to realize that direct use of many higher level cortical processes (for example, trying to tell yourself not to be afraid or arguing that there is no logical reason to be anxious) will not be as effective as making use of what we know about the language of the amygdala. *We need to speak the language of the amygdala if we want to reduce its influence on our anxiety.*

Can Anything Influence the Amygdala?

There is one part of our higher level cerebral cortex that does seem to have the ability to influence the amygdala. The **prefrontal cortex** is able to send signals to the central nucleus (the ignition switch) of the amygdala and to keep it from producing fear responses under certain conditions. We will have more to say about the role of the prefrontal cortex when we discuss exposure-based therapies, because these therapies seem to make use of the prefrontal areas of our brains. But in general, we should avoid trying to reason our amygdala out of the stress response once it has been initiated. Such attempts are like closing the barn door after the horse has left the barn. Once the stress response has been activated, our coping methods are somewhat limited.

The two best approaches to dealing with anxiety responses, given our knowledge of the nature of the stress response, are 1) to do whatever we can to avoid triggering the stress response whenever possible, and 2) when the stress response occurs, use strategies focused on modifying the physiological reactions directly. These two approaches are recommended especially for those who have difficulty with panic attacks, which are based on the same processes that create the Freeze/Fight/Flight response.

When Panic Attacks

A common difficulty faced by many individuals with anxiety disorders is the experience of a **panic attack**. A panic attack is caused by the sudden release of adrenaline or epinephrine into your system by your adrenal glands. As we have noted, the adrenal glands release the adrenaline in response to a signal from the amygdala. This can happen without involvement of the thinking areas of the brain, and that is why panic attacks seem to occur "out of the blue." They are periods of extreme terror accompanied by a pounding or racing heart, sweating, increased respiration, trembling or shaking, lightheadedness, and an overwhelming urge to flee. Other symptoms include nausea, numbness or tingling, a smothering sensation, tightness in the chest, feeling like you are unable to swallow, and hot flashes or chills. Because your pupils dilate, the world may seem unnaturally bright. One's sense of time may be altered. These symptoms are shared by other medical conditions, so be sure to consult a doctor to get a proper diagnosis.

Panic attacks are extremely distressing. Some people are afraid they are losing control, going crazy, or are about to die. The symptoms usually last from one to thirty minutes, but can return in waves. They are not only frightening, but quite exhausting.

A panic attack occurs when your body launches into the freeze/fight/flight mode for no apparent reason at all. Your body is immediately ready to defend itself physically or to escape, but there is no real danger. However, many times just having a panic attack feels dangerous in and of itself. The panic attack occurred because the amygdala sensed a cue or trigger of which you probably were not even aware, and instantly prepared your body for mortal combat. The trouble is that launching into the freeze/fight/flight response was a huge over-reaction by the amygdala since there was no danger present. (If there were some real danger, you would actually need the physical responses you are experiencing—to hide, run, or do battle—so your body's physical reactions would not be overblown. You would need all the strength and stamina you could muster!)

Since the amygdala is overreacting to some sort of cue when it initiates a panic attack, it is common to have panic attacks in the same or similar places repeatedly. This type of situational panic could occur in a crowd, while driving, at church, in a store, even while sleeping. Although the cue triggering the attack may be extremely difficult to pinpoint, it caught the attention of the amygdala, which set the panic attack in motion.

Most people have one or two panic attacks in their lifetime - and for most people, these incidents were just a frightening inconvenience. Individuals who have repeated panic attacks are often diagnosed with **panic disorder**. If the person begins to anticipate and fear having a panic attack, and avoids places where panic attacks have hit them in the past, they have symptoms of **agoraphobia** - a fear of fear. This is an extremely debilitating condition in which numerous places seem to be unsafe. By avoiding potentially panicky situations, these individuals shrink their world in a misguided attempt to protect themselves. Agoraphobia has the potential to confine people to their home, or even to one room within their home, if it gets out of control.

While it seems that panic attacks often come out of nowhere, the propensity for panic attacks does tend to run in families. This suggests that some of us have probably inherited amygdalas that are prone to react in this way. Also, significant life changes or stresses can bring on panic attacks in some people. These include graduation, job changes, a loss in the family, getting married or divorced, and other transitional events. Most panic attack sufferers are women, but that statistic may be due to under-reporting of panic attacks by men. Some people who have panic attacks try to cope in unhealthy ways, such as by drinking alcohol or using illegal drugs. These strategies may put a bandage on the problem, but they do not change the underlying circuitry of the brain in a helpful manner.

So, What to Do?

When you experience a panic attack, what is the best way to cope? What do you do if you are suddenly in the midst of a panic attack? What will work to calm you down?

One important thing to do when you are having a panic attack is to try to relax and to breathe s-l-o-w-l-y. Often the symptoms of panic attacks are directly related to **hyperventilation**, or breathing too quickly. Taking slow, full deep breaths that extend your diaphragm and chest outward is a good start. For some people, it helps to breathe for 6 to 10 breaths into a paper bag or even into cupped hands, because it increases the level of carbon dioxide in the air being inhaled. When a person hyperventilates, they throw off their oxygen/carbon dioxide balance and this can make them feel lightheaded. The danger of actually fainting is low, though, because there usually is no corresponding drop in blood pressure. (If you are prone to hyperventilation, you and your doctor might consider pulmonary function tests to make sure your lungs are working properly. Exercise can also help to improve lung function.)

Another helpful tip to remember when having a panic attack is to consciously relax your shoulders. The act of loosening your shoulder muscles will help you to calm down. Learning and diligently practicing relaxation techniques (See Chapter 7) will make this type of maneuver second nature. Feel free to wiggle your fingers and toes, or even to pace during a panic attack. These activities will burn off the excess adrenaline that is in your system.

Don't Make it Any Worse than It Is

Distraction is another wonderful tool to use against a panic attack. Because of the tendency to focus on one's symptoms, it is easy to make the panic attack worse by thinking about it. So, when you find yourself panicking, try to think of something else - anything else! Add numbers in your head. Name the objects around you that begin with the letter "t". Focus on music or news on the radio. Call a friend on your cell phone. Play a hand-held game. Do a puzzle. Eavesdrop on the people sitting next to you. Try anything to stop thinking about yourself and how you feel; such thoughts will only worsen and prolong the attack. Learning to control your thoughts - about yourself and about others - will help you tremendously. (See Chapter 10 for more suggestions.)

There is an inclination for people who have panic attacks to believe that everyone is looking at them, or that they will somehow embarrass themselves. Try not to second guess what other people are thinking. Most people probably are not aware of what is happening, or really don't care. And, if you do have someone around who is aware that you are having difficulty, tell them that a good way to assist you is to remind you to breathe slowly and to encourage you to think about something else. Even strike up a conversation with them to get your mind off of how you are feeling.

In a full blown panic attack, there are times when you are too panicky to think, and those are the times that the amygdala is taking charge and shutting out the influence of other parts of your brain. Just remember to breathe slowly, and eventually your anxiety will lessen. If a friend is present, the best way for them to help is to remind you to breathe deeply and to relax your muscles, which will be naturally tensing and tightening as your adrenaline surges. If your friend can distract you, you will probably be surprised at how much more quickly your level of anxiety decreases. In the meantime, focus on loosening your muscles and breathing slowly as you get through this difficult period.

Important Tips to Help You Get Past the Panic

One of the best ways to avoid having a panic attack is to stop worrying about panic attacks. Being preoccupied with panicking and constantly anticipating when or where a panic attack may occur makes another panic attack more likely. So, it is essential to keep from thinking too much about panicking or even about the symptoms of panicking. Focusing on a bodily sensation like your sweating palms or your thumping heart may lead to anxious feelings that can build into a panic attack.

Another important thing to remember about panic attacks is that when you do feel panicky, you need to resist the strong urge to flee the situation. While it is an extremely frightening and unpleasant experience, a panic attack will not physically hurt you. Escaping to safety may make you feel better in the short term, but in the long run, it will reinforce the power of the panic attacks and make them more difficult to overcome. If at all possible, try to relax, breathe deeply, and distract yourself during an attack. It is definitely easier said than done, but as you are learning to gain some control over your amygdala, it is the best advice to follow.

While all of this advice sounds very rational, unfortunately, your amygdala does not understand a word of it. For this reason, it is important for you and the rest of your brain to understand what is happening and why, and to take it to heart. Learning about the language of the amygdala will help you understand and modify what is happening when you have a panic attack. The knowledge that your amygdala is over-reacting to a trigger should help you to recognize that you are not in danger. It may be a very uncomfortable experience, but it is not causing you any harm.

Under no circumstances are you to listen to those individuals who tell you that "it is all in your head," or that you should "just get over it." *Panic attacks are an over-reaction by your amygdala. They are a biological disorder; they are not figments of your imagination.* Likewise, you cannot reason yourself out of them. Once your amygdala puts things in motion, you just have to sit tight and white-knuckle your way through - but you will get past the attack.

Next, we will show you how to use the language of the amygdala to teach your amygdala an alternative to anxiety. This process, which can change how the amygdala responds, is called exposure.

Chapter 5
Exposure-Based Treatment: Rewiring Your Brain

Using the Language of the Amygdala

Because the amygdala is so important in creating the emotional memories that cause fear and anxiety, knowing how to influence the amygdala is key in coping with anxiety disorders. What do we know about the amygdala that will assist us in modifying the emotional memories it creates?

We know that the language of the amygdala is one based on *associations* – the amygdala makes an association between events occurring one after another in time. We learn to fear the triggers that are associated with negative experiences, whether or not the triggers actually caused the negative experience. A survivor of a sexual assault, for example, may have a very strong emotional reaction to the smell of the specific cologne worn by the assailant, even though the cologne was irrelevant to the attack. Pairings of triggers with certain experiences are the most powerful influences in the language of the amygdala. *The amygdala needs to be shown new pairings through experience.* This is why thinking processes in higher levels of our cortex, like logic and reasoning, so often seem irrelevant when dealing with fear and anxiety. You cannot reason yourself out of anxiety very effectively because you are not speaking the right language to the amygdala.

In Chapter 3, we used the analogy of the "local" and the "express" lanes to describe how the amygdala can produce an emotional reaction before other parts of your brain even have time to process the information. Even though it is extremely quick, the amygdala's "express lane" creates emotional memories that have much more staying power than many of our other memories. Forgetting is a common characteristic of many of our conscious memories - we are all too familiar with lapses in memory that keep us from remembering a phone number or whether we took our medication with breakfast. In contrast, emotional memories created by the amygdala can seem indelible.

Another factor that adds to the complexity of working with emotional memories is that these memories can be formed and "recalled" by the amygdala outside of our awareness. This means that their influence can occur without our conscious knowledge. A variety of sensory experiences, even seemingly irrelevant cues that we barely notice in the situation, like a sound or a smell, can become connected to emotions. This makes triggers for anxiety difficult to pinpoint. To make matters worse, because the information processed by the amygdala (through the express lane) is not very detailed, the amygdala may respond to cues that are *similar to* the trigger—a process known as **generalization**. Thus, a timid child who became panicky after being forced to sit on Santa Claus's lap for a photo may later respond with anxiety to all bearded men.

Consider This:

Can you think of an example of generalization of fear in your life? Did your fear of a specific object ever generalize to other similar objects? Or did fear of a certain person generalize to other people who shared some characteristic with the person you feared?

In our amygdalas, anxiety becomes connected with certain triggers. Once such an association has formed, it appears very difficult, if not impossible, to erase this fear memory. We cannot break the connection the amygdala has formed, but we can develop *new* connections in the brain which *compete* with those that lead to fear and anxiety. The way to get the amygdala to create these new connections is to expose it to situations which contradict the connections it has made. If you show the amygdala new information that is inconsistent with what has been previously experienced, it will make new connections in response to this new information. It will learn from this new experience.

Exposure to new information allows you to rewire the brain in a way that will give you more control over your anxiety. Think of it as adding a "**bypass**" to the express lanes on the highway. When we create a new path and practice traveling it again and again, we establish an alternate route. Responding with fear and anxiety is no longer our only option! We can establish another *calmer* response as a way around our fear.

Exposure-Based Treatment

No other therapy for anxiety-based difficulties (especially panic attacks, phobias, and obsessive compulsive disorder) has had more dramatic success than **exposure-based treatment**.[1] In this approach, a person is "exposed" to the situation or object that he or she fears, sometimes in a gradual way and sometimes in a more abrupt manner. During each exposure, anxiety will rise – often to an uncomfortable level – and then it will begin to subside. The key is to let the anxiety run its course, peaking then lowering, without escaping the situation. In this way, the amygdala begins to learn that a previously feared situation is safe after all.

The power of exposure therapy lies in its ability to give the amygdala new experiences that prompt it to make new associations. According to psychologist Edna Foa, who has carried out extensive studies on the effectiveness of exposure, the power of exposure comes from the *corrective information* that exposure provides.[2] The amygdala is provided with experiences which show it that the triggers it previously associated with fear and anxiety are actually quite safe. Exposure-based treatment is a process of allowing the amygdala to learn safety in response to triggers that once evoked fear. Using exposure is one way to speak the language of the amygdala.

Systematic desensitization and flooding are two examples of exposure-based treatment. In **systematic desensitization**, you are taught relaxation strategies and encouraged to approach the feared object or situation in a gradual manner. Typically, this follows a slow but steady process that exposes you to situations that elicit more and more anxiety and fear as the therapy proceeds. Systematic desensitization makes use of gradual exposure, which is the kinder, gentler approach to exposure.

In contrast, during **flooding** a person is not exposed to the fear-eliciting situation in a gradual way, but jumps right in, so to speak. Exposure begins with the most fear-eliciting situation, and may last for hours. Flooding is more intense, but it also takes less time.

In either systematic desensitization or flooding, the feared situation may be presented, at least at first, by having the person imagine him or herself confronting the feared object or situation. Ultimately, the person will be asked to *directly experience* the feared situation, typically over and over. As a result of these experiences, the amygdala begins to re-wire itself by building new circuitry, "bypassing" the fear route. Each time the person is exposed to the situation and experiences a positive outcome, the bypass route becomes a deeper path. The more exposure is practiced, the more likely it is that the amygdala will choose the calm route over the fear route.

You may wonder whether a gradual approach, like desensitization, or a more rapid approach, like flooding, is more effective. First of all, for an approach to be effective, a person must be willing to use the approach. Anxious individuals tend to be more likely to try a gradual approach like desensitization, rather than flooding. In other words, desensitization has the advantage of being more user-friendly. But, research indicates that intense, extended presentation of cues associated with fear is more effective than a more gradual approach.[3]

If we consider the language of the amygdala, it seems that the amygdala is more likely to create new brain circuitry in response to intense presentation of new information, rather than in response to more gradually presented information. Perhaps flooding leads to better activation of the relevant circuitry. This does not mean that the amygdala will not learn as a result of systematic desensitization...just that it may take longer to translate the new experiences into new brain circuitry. So, when choosing between the approaches, you and your doctor or therapist should weigh the different advantages of each approach. Flooding is faster, but very intense. Systematic desensitization will take longer, but provides a gentler approach.

Have You Tried Exposure?

Exposure-based treatments are very effective, and, as a result, are one of the most frequently used approaches to reducing anxiety. Many individuals coping with anxiety have had some treatment focused on the use of exposure. If you have not had exposure-based treatment, we recommend that you seek a professional to guide you through this treatment, because evidence shows that it is very helpful. If you have already had exposure therapy, we are hopeful that reading this book will help you to understand why exposure works, or, perhaps, why the exposure treatment you had was not effective or lasting for some reason. Once you understand why the anxiety-producing centers in the brain respond so well to exposure, as well as what conditions tend to reduce the effectiveness of exposure, you may be more successful in taking advantage of the beneficial effects of exposure therapy.

One of the major goals of this book is to help you learn what brain processes can be modified to successfully control anxiety. When you consider what we know about the language of the amygdala, the effectiveness of exposure becomes apparent. Nothing speaks to the amygdala more clearly than experiences that activate neurons (nerve cells) associated with feared situations and objects. The amygdala is constantly monitoring the experiences you have and creating connections between neurons that reflect what is "safe" and what is "dangerous." This is the way that the amygdala learns through experience. Exposure-based treatment offers the amygdala the opportunity to make new connections and practice those connections over and over. As a result, exposure is one of the most effective methods for influencing the brain circuitry that gives rise to fear and anxiety.

Consider This:

Have you ever had experiences with exposure or exposure-based treatment? If so, how did you react to exposure and how did it influence your anxiety?

Extinction: Rewiring the Brain to Combat Fear

The process of using exposure to modify learned anxiety is called **extinction**. While exposure is what you are practicing as you confront a spider or an audience, "extinction" is the term used to describe what is happening to your fear or anxiety. Researchers will often use the phrase "extinguishing fear" when discussing the process of weakening a fear response. "Extinguishing fear" is such a comforting image. Wouldn't it be great if we had an "anxiety extinguisher" that we could spray on ourselves in order to put out our anxiety? Unfortunately, despite the compelling image, the process of trying to extinguish an anxiety response is more complex than one might expect. (Well, perhaps we should not be surprised by this, because if overcoming fear were simple and straightforward, so many people wouldn't be struggling with anxiety!)

The process of extinction is not as well understood as the process of acquiring fear or anxiety, but researchers are making headway. Through animal and human behavioral research, including research at the neurophysiological (cell) level, we have learned that extinction is not a matter of *unlearning* anxiety. Unfortunately, we cannot simply "disconnect" the connections that have been made between neurons by the amygdala; the process is somewhat more involved.

In order to modify emotional memories created by the amygdala, it is useful to think of them as links between memories that are based on connections between neurons. After a bad traffic accident, the conscious memory of the truck that hit you is connected with the emotional memory of the pain you experienced. As we discussed in Chapter 3, certain cues become triggers for anxiety because they have been associated with negative experiences. This means that anxiety becomes associated with certain cues because of processes that create strong connections between neurons.

Extinction does not eliminate the association made between certain experiences by severing the connections established between certain neurons. Instead, extinction is a separate process of making *new* connections that *compete with* the learned associations (neural connections) acquired in the past.[4] This is why we say that extinction is like building a "bypass" route around the express lane that leads to the anxiety response. Through the process of extinction, new circuitry is created in the amygdala. Extinction is about building new circuitry in the brain, rather than disconnecting the circuitry that already exists.

Back to Diagramming

If we return to our knowledge of classical conditioning and the diagrams with the boxes and arrows, we can see that the diagrams can also be used to explain extinction. See Figure 5.1, which illustrates the unfortunate experience of a young child who was scratched by a cat. The cat (originally a neutral object that becomes a Trigger) is paired with the scratch (Negative Event), which caused pain. As a result, the cat has come to elicit anxiety. When the child sees the cat, he experiences anxiety and is no longer interested in playing with the furry creature. How can this anxiety be "extinguished," as the scientists would say? How can the child make a bypass around his fear of the cat which was conditioned in his amygdala?

Figure5.1

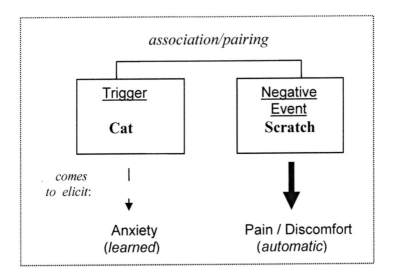

Activate to Generate!

Anxiety extinction does not come easily. *In order to extinguish anxiety, anxiety must be felt.* You may not realize this, but when you are feeling fear or anxiety, you are in the best position to rewire your brain to change that fear. Just as muscle will not become stronger if the fibers are not stressed through exercise, fear circuitry is impossible to modify without being activated. This activation takes place during exposure.

The process of extinction is often slowed down by the anxiety response itself. Imagine what happens when a person is exposed to an anxiety-eliciting situation, such as when a business woman with social anxiety disorder faces the prospect of speaking in public. When her anxiety increases, it creates an excellent opportunity for the process of extinction to begin. Unfortunately, her most likely reaction will probably be to avoid or escape such a situation. You can reason with her that she should face the situation, and she may even reason with herself. The amygdala is not operating on the basis of reason, however; it is simply activating established connections. The discomfort often seems unbearable, and the desire to escape, irresistible. If the business woman avoids the opportunity to speak, she will miss an opportunity to extinguish her anxiety. This vicious circle of experiencing anxiety, escaping anxiety, and thereby preserving anxiety is what makes anxiety reactions so difficult to modify. Anxiety can be self perpetuating!

Consider This:

Have you had experiences where you missed opportunities to overcome your anxiety because you avoided the situation that would have allowed you to do so?

We now know that the very activation of this circuitry holds the potential for the development of new connections between different neurons that will modify the amygdala's responses. We must **activate** the neurons **to generate** these connections. *We must press through the fear or anxiety to conquer it.* There was more than cowboy wisdom in the old adage "You gotta get back on the horse that threw you."

It may be helpful to remember the phrase **"Activate to Generate"** in order to understand why it is necessary to experience anxiety in order for extinction to occur. The activation of neurons in the amygdala underlies the effectiveness of exposure-based therapy. If you want to generate new connections in the brain, you must activate the circuits that store the memory of the feared object or situation.[5] Evidence shows that the people who benefit most from exposure are often the ones who have higher levels of emotional arousal during initial exposure experiences.[6] Perhaps this is why flooding works more rapidly than systematic desensitization.

Animal research and brain imaging indicate that the extinction process (experiencing a situation or object that causes you to feel anxiety while nothing negative happens) allows other portions of the brain to establish greater control over the amygdala's responding.[7] The anxiety learned in and stored by the amygdala is not erased, but other circuits are developed as new, calmer responses are conditioned. Such learning cannot occur without activating the circuitry that creates the anxiety. Because new connections cannot be formed unless the neurons are activated, we say you must *activate to generate* these connections.

An analogy may help you to remember the importance of activating the circuits, even though such activation is, to put it mildly, uncomfortable. When you are making a cup of tea, you will have better results if the water is hot (not necessarily boiling, according to tea connoisseurs, but "almost" boiling). Placing tea leaves or a teabag in a cup of cold water will not allow the flavor of the tea leaves to be infused into the water. Hot water is needed for flavor extraction. In a similar way, our neural circuits need to be activated (or hot) for them to make new connections. So, when it comes to anxiety, we need to be exposed to the heat if we want to rewire our neural circuitry.

How Does Anxiety Extinction Occur in the Brain?

Neurological research has proposed tentative answers to the question of how extinction occurs in the brain only in the past ten or so years. As we've discussed, the neural circuits in the amygdala that store information about a feared object or situation must be *activated* for extinction to take place. The individual must be exposed to the trigger to activate the relevant neurons if rewiring is to occur. Unfortunately, when these neurons are activated, it is likely that other neurons associated with anxiety responses, including the freeze/fight/flight response, also become activated.

In other words, during exposure, the individual is likely to be experiencing anxiety and feeling a strong impulse to escape. This is why exposure therapy can be difficult to undertake. It is scary. But you must feel the anxiety in order to build a bypass around it. Naturally, most of us do not lightheartedly seek the type of situation that we are describing: we want to avoid situations in which objects (such as bridges) or events (such as flying on an airplane) elicit anxiety and fear responses. Because asking you to deliberately seek out anxiety-provoking experiences is demanding and challenging, it is helpful for you to know that these processes are required to rewire the brain and allow extinction to occur. Understanding how and why these processes work can help you and your doctor or therapist to design exposure experiences that are more productive. Knowing what you are attempting to accomplish in your brain may make the stress of the experience more tolerable, too.

Exposure is a "no pain, no gain" situation. In order for your brain to have an option besides the "express" route to take, you must expose yourself to the situation and allow yourself to experience anxiety and fear. The optimal condition for the most learning to take place in the brain is when the neurons are excited, just as the optimal condition for building muscle mass in the body is when the muscle fibers are fatigued. In a parallel way, as you do more repetitions, you grow stronger, mentally and physically. You can think of exposure as a way of providing new exercises for your amygdala.

So, if we take the example of a child who has acquired a fear of a cat, we will want to expose him to a friendly cat in order to extinguish his fear. When the child sees or touches the cat under positive circumstances (while petting it and enjoying its softness, being amused by its antics, etc.), the amygdala can be stimulated to establish new associations with the cat. The more the child interacts with the cat in a positive way, the stronger the new associations will become, and the more anxiety will be reduced. With repeated exposure to a friendly cat, the child's amygdala will create a bypass around his fear and anxiety.

Exposure, whether gradual or sudden, is not easy. During exposure, the child is likely to be feeling and expressing fear of the cat. But this exposure is necessary if we are to activate the neurons we wish to rewire. There is no way to change the connections the amygdala has created about cats without giving the amygdala new experiences with a cat, and, as a consequence, creating some anxiety. In fact, feeling anxiety is a good indication that the correct circuits in the brain have been activated and are ready for new learning.

To diagram the process of creating new connections, we could build onto the previous diagram, Figure 5.1. This time, in Figure 5.2, we link the cat, not with a scratch, but with a positive experience, such as watching playful chasing of a string or petting a purring cat. With these positive experiences, the cat will come to elicit more positive feelings of calmness or pleasure. The new connection can *compete* with the previous connection between the cat and anxiety and become a route around the anxiety response. The more the child is exposed to this bypass, the more worn the path will become and the more likely it is that he will feel positive emotions (calmness, amusement) rather than anxiety when he encounters cats in the future. Repeated exposure creates this new alternative response.

Figure 5.2

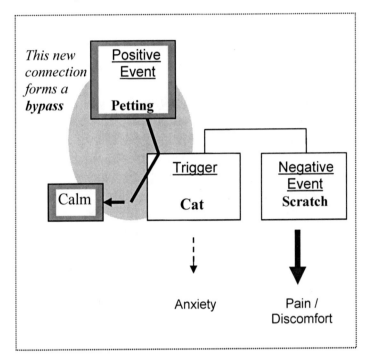

Take the Plunge

We recognize that exposure-based approaches are not pleasant or easy. It is difficult to deliberately put yourself in a situation designed by its very nature to distress you. But we can assure you that a great deal of evidence indicates that exposure is a very effective way of changing the connections in your brain that are responsible for the anxiety you experience. All the same, it is difficult - and some days, downright impossible - to put yourself through such an experience. Exposure is not something you should approach lightly, because it is possible to *strengthen* anxiety if the person escapes from the exposure situation before their anxiety is reduced. If you escape, rather than stick to the exposure process, you can reinforce the anxiety response and not bypass the anxiety circuitry at all. You need to stay in the situation until your anxiety decreases, preferably by half.

Because of these potential drawbacks, we recommend that you work with a professional therapist to get the best exposure-based treatment. You also should carefully choose when to use exposure (and when not to use it), so that you can utilize this powerful tool to help you gain control over the most important aspects of your life. In later chapters, we will discuss methods to help you identify the situations in which you will benefit from exposure, and when exposure is not necessary.

In order to understand the transformative power of exposure, consider the analogy of taking a swim. Have you ever dipped your toes into a pool or lake, and winced upon feeling the cold water? As you wade farther in, you are aware of the water's chilly temperature as it gradually reaches your stomach and chest. After a period of time, however, your body adjusts, and you find yourself comfortable in the water. You smile at the others on the shore who are up to their knees and complaining "It's cold!" The same process of adjustment occurs with exposure. Your brain will adapt if you remain in the situation. When you feel your anxiety decrease while you are practicing exposure, know that the change you are making in your brain is one that will last!

Consider This:

Have you ever put yourself through an experience that was difficult or painful, in order to accomplish something that was important to you? Did it involve a great deal of effort, and perhaps physical pain? Childbirth is a common experience mentioned by women, for example.

Creating New Connections

Now you know that most researchers currently believe that extinction of anxiety results from a learning process that does not erase anxiety, but instead *competes with* the anxiety that was previously learned. When we use exposure, our goal is to build new connections in the brain that will compete with the connections that give rise to anxiety. Not only do we want to form these new connections, but we also want to practice them repeatedly so that they become strong enough to override the fear circuitry being activated in the amygdala. We want to create another path for the impulses to travel, instead of the fear/anxiety route.

So remember, to effectively create new connections, you must expose yourself repeatedly to the cues that cause you to feel anxiety, making sure that you *activate* the fear circuitry so that you can *generate* new connections. The other essential goal is to ensure that the new emotions that you experience during exposure are neutral or positive ones. If you are trying to extinguish a fear of elevators, spend time riding in elevators, and make sure that your experiences are uneventful, calm or even pleasant. The most effective extinction will occur if you expose yourself to a variety of elevators in different settings, using generalization to your advantage.

During exposure, it is also vital that you do not leave the situation in fear. Escaping in this way will only strengthen the fear circuitry. Do not leave the situation until you feel your anxiety decrease substantially. Your amygdala needs to learn that it is safe to be in and around elevators, and that escape is not necessary. The amygdala only learns through experience.

Understanding how the brain creates a bypass around fear is powerful knowledge to use in rewiring your brain to overcome anxiety. In Chapter 8, we will return to exposure-based treatment, and provide specific instructions for designing effective exposure exercises. This includes ways to identify the important triggers that you need to take into account for the exercises to be productive. But first, we will discuss some specific factors that can influence the effectiveness of exposure.

Chapter 6
Exposure-Based Treatment:
Factors to Consider

Exposure: It Ain't Easy!

Exposure-based treatment is not a pleasant experience. You know at the outset that you are going to experience anxiety and fear, and that you will feel the desire to escape. When you are placing yourself in such a difficult situation, you want to be assured that it will be effective. Why put yourself through a stressful experience if it will not have some long-term benefit?

We speak from experience when we say that, personally, we are more willing to endure distressing experiences when we know that they will lead to some lasting improvement. If there are ways to make the experience more effective at creating lasting change, we definitely want you to know about them. Similarly, if there are some factors that will undermine the effectiveness of the exposure, making your efforts less successful, we want you to know about these factors, too.

In this chapter, we explain more of the specifics about the process of extinction, and identify factors that tend to interfere with what you are trying to accomplish during exposure-based treatment. We'll give you examples of what works, and what does not. This information will help you and your doctor or therapist to design effective exposure experiences. It also may explain why exposure experiences may not have been very helpful for you in the past if you attempted them.

Extinction Learned Just Like Anxiety? Nope.

The truth is that there are some important distinctions between the processes of learning fear and of learning extinction. In the brain, the process of learning new, competing connections (extinction) is more complicated than learning anxiety because different structures, different neurotransmitters, different neurons, and different types of molecules in the neurons themselves are involved. Without going into a lot of detail about the specifics, we want to give you enough information about the process to help you to be more effective in extinguishing your fear and anxiety.

First of all, the process of learning extinction takes more time than does the process of acquiring fear. Our brains are prepared to learn fears, anxiety, and avoidance behaviors very quickly, with few "practice trials" required. This is probably because our ancestors were those individuals who learned to be afraid and escape after only one or two experiences in a dangerous situation. Overly confident individuals who needed multiple learning experiences to become fearful may not have survived to pass on their genes or to protect their offspring. As a result, we end up with humans who have a strong tendency to become anxious.

While it was clearly more adaptive for our ancestors to learn to be afraid quickly, it was *not* adaptive to learn to overcome their fears too quickly. Thus, the process of learning *not* to respond fearfully takes longer and is also more easily forgotten. Research clearly shows that extinction is more easily forgotten than fear.[1] The brain's bias in favor of holding on to fear-related memories appears to be an evolutionary advantage.

This means that in order to keep extinction memories strong, you not only need to establish them through exposure, but you need to *keep practicing* them so that they are not forgotten. Just as your tennis backhand will get rusty if you don't use it, you need to maintain your confidence in coping with a fear-provoking experience by repeatedly practicing exposure. Successful exposure experiences help to make the calmer "bypass" route an alternative to the amygdala's fear conditioning.

Let's say, for example, that you want to extinguish an anxiety response associated with driving in busy highway traffic. Each time you drive on the congested interstate, you strengthen the emotional memory that links this driving experience with calm responding. If you do not drive it for a couple of weeks, your fear may be a little higher the next time you merge into the traffic. The more you regularly practice exposure, the stronger the extinction memory becomes, and the less likely it is that forgetting the extinction "bypass" will begin.

Second, the process of extinction is more complicated than is the process of learning fear. Recent animal studies as well as brain imaging research show that the process of extinction requires more circuits in the brain than does the process of learning

fear.[2] Perhaps this is why extinction is easier to disrupt
or forget. The involvement of more circuits offers more
opportunities for the neurons to fail to respond
somewhere along the pathway. In contrast, fear
responding is streamlined (the express lane) and
involves fewer circuits, so it is more rapid and direct.
The evolutionary advantages to this type of wiring seem
clear. Simple, streamlined circuitry means quicker
responding that can mean the difference between life
and death. But for those of us trying to combat anxiety
reactions, it also means that the brain is biased in favor
of preserving fear.

So, there is a good reason why the process of
rewiring our brains to minimize fear and anxiety
responses can seem like an uphill battle - there is more
extensive circuitry involved. This means that you need
to have patience with your brain as it learns to
overcome fear. It may take longer than you would like,
but your brain will learn.

Another interesting difference is that the brain
creates extinction memories differently than fear
memories.[3] Fear memories seem to be created and
stored by the amygdala itself, but when extinction is
learned, activation also occurs in a part of the cerebral
cortex known as the **prefrontal cortex**. The
prefrontal cortex has neurons that send messages to
the amygdala that inhibit fear responses. After
extinction, it is apparently the prefrontal cortex that
stores the memories that link the feared object or
situation with more positive responding. The amygdala
continues to be activated by the previously established
fear circuitry, but now there is also a *competing*

process stored in the prefrontal cortex that can inhibit the central amygdala.

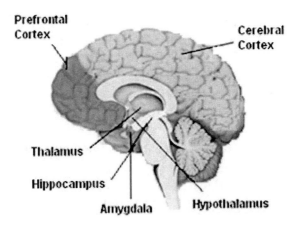

In other words, memories for fear or anxiety continue to exist alongside the new memories you create through exposure to help you overcome fear. The anxiety memories are probably always present, ready to be reactivated, so you need to keep exposing yourself to the feared situation in order to keep your anxiety at bay. If there is a situation or object that your amygdala sees as dangerous, repeated experiences with that situation or object are the best way to keep your anxiety under control. You need to keep reminding your amygdala that you are safe!

Consider This:

Have you ever felt that getting rid of your fears was an uphill battle? Could you feel your brain holding on to your fears despite your efforts to change? Does this section of the book help to explain why you felt this way? Does it give you suggestions about how to be more successful at changing your brain to resist fears and anxiety?

Third, context matters. The context in which a person is exposed to a feared object or situation also seems to have a big impact upon which memory is more likely to be activated in the person's amygdala. [4] **Context** refers to the situation or setting in which the exposure to the feared object or event is happening. It seems that, after extinction, putting the person in a context other than the one in which extinction occurred makes it more likely that fear will resurface.[5] For example, repeated exposure to an elevator at work may reduce a person's fear of this elevator, and perhaps even other elevators in the same building. But if an elevator is encountered in a different building, the neural connection eliciting fear may be more activated than the bypass leading to calm responding. Fearful responding could be stronger than calm responding in this new context. It can be very confusing when fear returns in this manner. You might think "Didn't I get past this fear?" Unfortunately, it seems that our brains are very sensitive to the situation in which we are exposed to what we fear, so there may be a return of fear when the feared object or event is encountered in a different context.

For this reason, if you are trying to extinguish a fear of dogs, for example, it is important to be exposed to a variety of dogs in a variety of situations in order to effectively reduce your fear. If you only encounter a specific dog in a specific location, your fear will definitely be reduced in that situation, as long as your experiences with the dog are positive ones. In other situations, however, you may find yourself as fearful of dogs as you once were. If you spend time with different dogs in a variety of locations, the reduction in your fear is more likely to **generalize** across situations. So consider the context in which you are planning to extinguish your fears, and vary the context to make exposure more effective. Then, when you encounter a dog in a new situation, you will be less likely to experience a great deal of fear or anxiety.

A Caution about Medication

We will discuss medications in more depth in Chapter 9, but here we should note that medications can affect the process of exposure. Some medications called benzodiazepines, including Valium, Xanax, and Klonopin, might impair the learning process.[6] While these medications help us feel better in the short-term, reducing anxiety by reducing the activation of neurons, they also make it more difficult for these neurons to learn new connections. This means that some medications could impair the learning of new associations (the bypass route) that would result in extinction. The medications might actually impair the long-term change in anxiety that we are working toward.

So, you and your doctor should consider the medications you are on when you are undergoing exposure-based treatment. Benzodiazepines are useful for short-term relief of anxiety, but they are not likely to result in permanent changes in the brain that will reduce anxiety in the long-term. Remember that you need to *activate* the fear circuitry if you are going to *generate* new learning. Medications that minimize the activation of your anxiety responses help you to feel better, but they may prevent your brain from creating the new circuitry that promotes extinction. If you are going to put yourself through the difficult process of exposure, you want to make sure that you aren't taking a medication that will keep exposure from having lasting beneficial effects.

On the other hand, medications that promote the development of new connections in the brain, SSRIs like Prosac, Zoloft, Celexa, and Lexapro, may be helpful in the process of retraining the brain. Although we are not sure how the SSRIs specifically affect the process of extinguishing fear, it seems that the increased flexibility they promote in the brain may facilitate new learning. These medications are more likely to be helpful in the process of exposure, perhaps because they help the brain make new connections. A particular medication, D-cycloserine, has recently been found to seemingly increase the amygdala's ability to learn the extinction of anxiety. We will discuss the promise of this medication in Chapter 9.

In summary, you may want to review with your doctor the medications you are taking, and to ask about their impact on the exposure process. Remember that you should always consult with your doctor before contemplating any changes in your medication. Do not try to manage your medications without medical supervision.

The Danger of Safety

When designing opportunities for exposure-based experiences, you should also be aware of the role of **safety-seeking behaviors**. Safety-seeking behaviors are behaviors that individuals often engage in when they are faced with a fear-provoking situation. For example, people who have social phobia may avoid eye contact with others or place their hands in their pockets when they are in social situations. Safety-seeking behaviors can be as simple as fiddling with one's watch, or as complicated as making sure that a specific person is always at your side in a particular situation. These behaviors serve the purpose of increasing the person's feelings of safety and comfort in the situation. They seem innocent enough, and in fact can be helpful in getting through a difficult situation - in the short run. But surprisingly, the use of these behaviors has been shown to interfere with the effectiveness of exposure,[7] so it is important to be aware of safety-seeking behaviors when you are planning to use exposure to reduce your anxiety.

So, let's be clear about what safety-seeking behaviors are and how to identify them. Safety-seeking behaviors are avoidance responses. They are responses that are performed to *prevent* a perceived danger. When you carry them out, they help you to feel safer in some way by making you feel reassured that danger is less likely. Most people who have dealt with chronic anxiety are aware of their own safety-seeking behaviors. For example, if you ask a woman with agoraphobia why she is gripping the steering wheel tightly with both hands, and she says that this gripping makes it less likely that she will have an accident, then the gripping is a safety-seeking behavior.

Safety-seeking behaviors differ from **coping responses**, which are responses to *reduce* the anxiety itself, rather than to prevent danger. Coping responses are not performed to avoid a feared catastrophe, but only to ease anxiety. Making reassuring statements to yourself, such as "Everything will be all right," or trying to relax the tension in your muscles are typical coping responses.

Differentiating between coping responses (which do not seem to decrease the effectiveness of exposure) and safety-seeking behaviors (which undermine the effectiveness of exposure) can be difficult. Sometimes the behaviors seem very similar, but the key difference is whether the person believes that the behavior is preventing a catastrophe from occurring.[8] If a person is breathing deeply in order to reduce her anxiety while she thinks about spiders, this is a coping response; but, if she is breathing deeply more to focus on her breathing than to actually think about spiders, this is a safety-seeking behavior.

The following questions are designed to help you to detect a safety-seeking behavior so that you can eliminate it.

- What do you think would happen if you didn't do this behavior?
- What are you avoiding by doing the behavior?
  If you are trying to avoid a certain outcome, and not just trying to reduce

anxiety, this is probably a safety-seeking behavior.
- Do you need to do this every time you are in the situation?
- Does the behavior prevent you from accomplishing what you want/need to do?
If the answer to these questions is YES, this is probably a safety-seeking behavior.

Safety-seeking behaviors are designed to do just that – to increase a person's feeling of safety. If a person says "I have to sit facing the door when I am in a restaurant so that I can see the exit," the person is engaging in a safety-seeking behavior. Many compulsions performed by individuals with obsessive compulsive disorder can be seen as safety-seeking behaviors. A woman who has to repeatedly check her stove before leaving the house is engaging in a safety-seeking behavior that helps her feel more secure. It is useful if you can identify your own safety-seeking behaviors and take care not to use them during exposure sessions to get the most benefit.

Consider This:

What do you worry about happening in anxiety-provoking situations? Are there certain catastrophic events you think about? Are there any safety-seeking behaviors that you perform that are related to avoiding these events? Try to identify safety-seeking behaviors that you are likely to use in anxiety provoking situations.

Why is Safety-seeking a Problem?

Studies repeatedly show that exposure will be more effective in eliminating anxiety if safety-seeking behaviors are not performed during exposure.[9] Why is it that safety-seeking behaviors interfere with the effectiveness of exposure? There are a variety of theories about this, but no specific answer has been accepted at this time.[10] Perhaps a person using safety-seeking behaviors feels protected from the perceived danger in some way, and this makes exposure less effective. If a person believes that having medication in her pocket allows her to avoid having a panic attack, the medication may prevent her from truly facing her fear that being in a movie theatre may provoke a panic attack. She may believe that, as long as she has the medication in her pocket, she is protected from the panic attack. Even though she completes exposure sessions in the theatre, return of fear is likely if she faces the same situation without her medication available.

On the other hand, it may be that the focus on safety-seeking behaviors distracts the person from the situation that is associated with anxiety, keeping the person's attention on other, less threatening aspects of the situation. Consider a man who fears eating in front of others and who practices eating with friends while engaging in the safety-seeking behavior of frequently drinking water. The man may be paying so much attention to drinking his water that he avoids focusing on the fear-eliciting aspects of the situation, such as making eye contact and talking with others. Since the man does not pay attention to fear-provoking activities during the exposure, his fear does not extinguish as effectively.

Although we do not yet know for certain what neurological processes cause safety-seeking behavior to undermine extinction, we know that the brain is very sensitive to context. Use of safety signals may mean that exposure occurs in a specific context (when the safety signal is present) and that fear will return when the individual is presented with a different context (when the safety signal is missing).

We also know that the process of extinction requires adequate activation of neurons associated with cues in fear-provoking situations. Perhaps safety-seeking behaviors keep the person from adequately focusing on cues that elicit anxiety, and not enough activation of the brain's circuitry occurs. Remember, we must *activate to generate* new connections! Studies indicate that the more that a person focuses on the threat experienced during exposure, rather than distracting him or herself, the more effective the exposure will be in reducing anxiety.[11]

Giving up safety-seeking behaviors can be a challenge, but if you are making the effort to use exposure-based treatment, you want it to be effective. We have good reason to recommend that you avoid safety-seeking behaviors when using exposure-based treatment; exposure exercises are more effective when you eliminate these behaviors.

Keeping Extinction Memories Fresh

Perhaps because extinction memories require more extensive connections in the brain, they are more subject to disruption and loss. We have stressed that reminder experiences are often helpful in keeping extinction memories alive. Once a boy has shown signs of overcoming his fear of dogs, it is easy to assume the fear is gone, but extinction will be maintained more effectively if, every once in a while, you insure that the boy is exposed to a friendly dog. This keeps the extinction memory fresh. The reverse is also true: a new experience with a threatening dog will strengthen the fear circuitry, and extinction may seem to have disappeared. Extinction has not disappeared, but it will need to be reestablished, however, because fear is so readily learned. Note that extinction will be learned more quickly the next time; this demonstrates that the extinction circuitry is still in place, but just needs to be strengthened. Practice and repetition are valuable tools to use in the process of extinction.

Sometimes it is useful to think of the extinction process as creating a new path in the brain. Just as when you create a path through a wooded forest, you need to keep traveling that path so that it does not become overgrown and lost. The more times you use the path (the bypass), the more you maintain it as a viable route for the brain to use.

In Summary

Hopefully, you now understand the value of knowing the language of the amygdala when you use exposure-based treatment. Comprehending the nature of the brain circuitry underlying the processes of fear conditioning and extinction can help you to recognize why anxiety is so difficult to eliminate. It can also assist you and your therapist in designing exposure exercises which create new connections that compete with your fear responses.

You cannot consciously tell yourself to overcome your fears and expect rewiring of neural circuits to result, because the amygdala needs *experience* to learn. But you can design exposure experiences that allow you to rewire your brain circuitry. We would never characterize the process as simple or easy. It can be a slow and frightening; but, it is predictable - and best of all, **it does work.**

Chapter 7
Relaxation and Exercise

Take a Breath Now!

Does all this discussion about exposure motivate you to try some exposure exercises? Or, perhaps it has you feeling somewhat cautious about proceeding? In this chapter, we take a break before moving on to how to design exposure exercises...and for a very good reason. As you approach a stressful situation, you should know what is likely to occur and know some ways to cope with the anxiety which you will experience. So here we highlight the importance of relaxation, which can be extremely useful during exposure. We will also share the benefits of exercise in coping with the freeze/fight/flight response. Read this chapter carefully, because it is important in a whole brain approach to anxiety!

Coping with the Freeze/Fight/Flight Response

When you attempt to use exposure, your body will respond in a fairly predictable way, and it won't be pleasant; you will get anxious. We all experience a similarly programmed stress response when our amygdala believes we are threatened. As we noted in Chapter 4, the amygdala can instantly increase heart rate and blood pressure, quicken our breathing, direct blood flow to our extremities, and slow our digestive processes. These physiological changes occur because of the activation of the **sympathetic nervous system**, and they can be initiated without any deliberate effort on our part. Once again, it is important to note that these spontaneously activated processes, whether described as the fear response, anxiety, or stress, result from brain activities that are not in our conscious awareness.

Lack of conscious awareness does not mean that we have a complete lack of control over these processes, however. Although we do not consciously control the rate of our breathing most of the time, for example, we are capable of deliberately modifying it when we hold our breath. A variety of techniques have been developed for activating the **parasympathetic nervous system**, which reverses some of the effects of the sympathetic nervous system. The parasympathetic system is responsible for resting and digestion. It slows down heart rate and increases intestinal as well as glandular activity. This system is more likely to be activated when a person is relaxed, and those professionals who treat anxiety[1] often encourage individuals to engage in activities that decrease sympathetic activation (accelerating) and strengthen the tendency toward parasympathetic activation (braking). Relaxation training is one of the primary methods suggested for facilitating parasympathetic activation.

Some functions of the sympathetic and parasympathetic branches of the nervous system appear on the next page.

Sympathetic		Parasympathetic
Dilates pupils		Constricts pupils
Decreases saliva		Increases saliva
Accelerates breathing		Slows breathing
Accelerates heart		Slows heart
Slows digestion		Stimulates digestion
Releases adrenaline		
Relaxes bladder		Contracts bladder
Contracts anus		Relaxes anus

Relaxation training has been formally used since Edmund Jacobson[2] developed a process called Progressive Muscle Relaxation in the 1930s. A variety of approaches have been developed, but most approaches focus on two physical processes: breathing and relaxing one's muscles. Different people will respond in their own ways to different relaxation strategies, but virtually everyone can find some benefit from the process of relaxation training. Relaxation can be used in many situations and has been shown to have beneficial effects, especially in the short-term. Relaxation is also an integral part of more complex approaches to reducing stress and anxiety, such as meditation and yoga.

Like a Breath of Fresh Air

If you take a few moments right now and attend to your breathing, you may be able to demonstrate to yourself some of the basic effects of relaxation. Take a deep breath. Make a point of expanding your lungs as you inhale deeply and slowly. Don't hold your breath. Allow yourself to exhale naturally. Take a couple more deep slow breaths, exhaling naturally. Some people feel a change in their level of anxiety almost immediately. We seldom are aware that we frequently hold our breath, or breathe shallowly. Simply providing your body with ample oxygen by breathing in a slow, deep manner can be calming and stress-relieving.

Consider This:

Take a few deep breaths. Inhale slowly and deeply, and exhale fully. Do not force your breathing. Breathe gently both in and out. Don't worry about whether or not you are breathing through your mouth or nose—just breathe in a comfortable manner. Note how the deliberate attempt to slow and deepen your breathing affects you. Does it have a calming effect for you?

Note that not everyone finds slowing and deepening their breathing to be calming. Increased attention to breathing can increase anxiety in some people, especially when an individual has asthma or other breathing difficulties. In that case, a person may benefit from relaxation strategies that focus on reducing muscle tension, or strategies that make use of music or movement. But, many people are surprised that simple breathing exercises can reduce anxiety and increase calmness almost immediately.

How Does Breathing Affect the Body?

When an individual is anxious, he or she is likely to breathe quickly and shallowly. The person may not get enough oxygen, which produces an uncomfortable sensation. When a person breathes too quickly and shallowly, **hyperventilation** can occur. Usually hyperventilation occurs when a person expels carbon dioxide too quickly, causing in low levels of carbon dioxide in the blood. This can result in a feeling of tingling in the hands, feet, or face, dizziness, belching, or a feeling of unreality or confusion. Often people attribute dizziness or tingling to anxiety, when what they actually are experiencing are the effects of hyperventilation. Their symptoms can be reduced simply by attending to more healthy breathing practices. People who are hyperventilating usually are instructed to breathe into a paper bag. The bag captures the carbon dioxide when they exhale, which in turn increases the amount inhaled and replaced in the blood stream. It is a very effective method of reversing lightheadedness and other symptoms.

A specific method of breathing known as **diaphragmatic** or **abdominal breathing** is recommended for activating the parasympathetic nervous system.[3] This type of breathing helps to turn on a "relaxation response" in the body. In this type of breathing, a person breathes more from the abdomen than from the chest. The corresponding movement of the diaphragm (the muscle under the lungs) has a massaging effect on the liver, stomach, and even the heart. This deeper, diaphragmatic breathing is thought to have beneficial effects on many of these internal organs.

Consider This:

As you are sitting, place one hand on your chest, and one hand on your stomach. Take a deep breath, and see what part of your body expands. Effective diaphragmatic breathing will cause your stomach to expand as you inhale, and retract as you exhale. Your chest should not move much at all. Try to focus on breathing deeply in a manner that expands your stomach as you fill your lungs with air. Too many of us pull in our stomachs as we inhale. This keeps the diaphragm from expanding downward effectively.

Healthy breathing techniques can become second nature with practice. Pay attention to your style and pattern of breathing and consciously modify it. Practicing for five minute sessions at least three times a day can increase your awareness of your breathing practices, as well as train you to have more effective breathing habits. Try to be aware of when you tend to hold your breath, breathe shallowly, or hyperventilate, and make a conscious effort to modify your breathing to establish a healthy breathing pattern. With practice, you will find that diaphragmatic breathing becomes second nature, and that many symptoms that you may have considered part of your anxiety can be alleviated.

Sometimes we try to tell ourselves to calm down, and try to "think" ourselves into relaxing. After reading this section, we hope you see another approach. Instead of focusing on your thoughts (the cerebral cortex approach), focus directly on the physiological responses that the amygdala is turning on, and try to counter them with parasympathetic activation. Slower breathing will send a message directly to the amygdala that the body is calming down; this is more likely to affect the amygdala's responding than all the "thinking" you can do.

What are Your Muscles Doing?

The second component of most relaxation training programs is muscle relaxation. Muscle relaxation also works to counter the stress-related activation of the sympathetic nervous system. Relaxing your muscles can strengthen parasympathetic responding, too.

The sympathetic nervous system creates increased muscle tension because fibers in the sympathetic nervous system activate muscles needed when we are in danger. Our sympathetic nervous system developed to help us cope with the stresses in our lives, but it is programmed to prepare us to fight or flee. The problems we face in today's world are seldom ones that we can fight or run from. Nonetheless, muscle tension is apparently programmed into us.

We often are completely unaware of the muscle tension that builds up in our bodies on a daily basis. If you observe yourself, you may find that you are clenching your teeth or tensing your stomach muscles for no apparent reason. Certain areas of the body seem to be vulnerable repositories for stress, including the jaw, forehead, shoulders, back, and neck. Constant muscle tension uses energy and can leave a person feeling stiff and exhausted at the end of the day. The first step in reducing muscle tension is to discover which areas you tend to tense up. Taking a brief inventory of areas that are most susceptible to muscle tension is a useful exercise.

Consider This:

Determine whether muscle tension is present in the areas of the body that are particularly vulnerable to stress. At this moment, check your jaw, tongue, and lips to see if they are relaxed or tense. Consider whether muscle tension is tightening your forehead. Determine whether your shoulders are loose, low, and relaxed, or if they are tightened up toward your ears. Some people tense their stomach as though expecting to be punched any moment. Others clench their fists or curl their toes. Take a brief inventory to see where you are holding your tension at this moment.

Once you have an idea of the areas in your body that are vulnerable to muscle tension, you are ready to learn to relax those areas. First, it may help to experience the difference between the feelings of muscle tension and relaxation. Tension is often experienced as a tight or strained feeling. In contrast, relaxation is often described as a loose and heavy feeling.

Consider This:

Make a fist with one of your hands, and clench it tightly while you count to 10. Then let that hand relax by dropping it limply into your lap or onto another surface. Compare the feeling of tension that you experienced as you clenched your fist to the feeling of relaxation while the muscles are loose and limp. Do you recognize a difference? Compare the hand that you tightened and relaxed to the hand that you did not use. Notice whether one hand feels more relaxed than the other. Often tensing and releasing muscles helps to create a feeling of relaxation in those muscles.

Progressive Muscle Relaxation

One of the most popular muscle relaxation techniques involves focusing on one muscle group at a time. A person briefly tenses then relaxes the muscles in that group, then switches from that group to the next, until all major muscle groups are relaxed. This type of relaxation is called **Progressive Muscle Relaxation**.[4] When you first learn Progressive Muscle Relaxation, it may take you 30 minutes or longer to complete the entire process of relaxing every muscle group. With time and practice, you can train yourself to relax your muscles more readily and much less time is required. If practiced diligently, a satisfying level of relaxation often can be achieved in less than five minutes.

A list of the major muscle groups, in the recommended order for relaxing muscles, is printed below. Practice using this list to relax yourself at least two times a day until you have reduced the time it takes to achieve relaxation to approximately ten minutes. Typically, a person eventually will learn to relax most of his or her muscles without having to tense them first, and may need only tense those stubborn groups of muscles that seem particularly vulnerable to retaining stress. For each person, a different group of muscles may resist relaxation. Learning to relax effectively is an individual process that must be tailored to each person with his or her specific needs in mind. We recommend that you try a variety of approaches, and choose the one that is most effective for you.

Suggested Order of Muscle Groups to Focus on in Progressive Muscle Relaxation

- Hands, forearms, biceps
- Feet, calves, thighs, buttocks
- Forehead, jaw, lips, tongue
- Neck, shoulders
- Stomach

Consider Different Strategies for Relaxation

It is essential that you know yourself well enough to select the relaxation strategy that is most useful to you. Progressive Muscle Relaxation is not the only approach that allows a person to achieve relaxation; experimenting with different approaches is recommended. Tensing muscles is not always required to achieve relaxation. In fact, if a person has an injury or chronic pain difficulties, tensing muscles may be counterproductive. In Appendix B, you will find instructions for relaxation *with* and *without* a focus on creating muscle tension as a part of the process. Even if you start with Progressive Muscle Relaxation, once you master the process of relaxing your muscles, you may change to a tension-free approach because it is more efficient.

Imagery is also a beneficial relaxation strategy. Some individuals have the ability to imagine themselves in another location and can use visualization to effectively attain a relaxed state. If you are one of those individuals, you may find that imagining yourself on a beach or in a peaceful forest glade allows you to achieve a more satisfying state of relaxation than does a focus on muscle relaxation. In Appendix C, you will find a sample set of instructions for guided imagery.

Consider This:

To assess your ability to use imagery, take a few moments to close your eyes, and imagine yourself in the relaxing setting described below. After this exercise, consider how well you were able to imagine yourself in the described setting. If such an experiment comes readily to you, and you find it pleasant and engaging, the use of imagery is highly recommended. If it is difficult and you find your mind wandering, then you will probably find other strategies more effective.

> *Imagine yourself on a warm beach. Feel the sun warming your skin, and the cool breeze coming off the water. Listen to the sounds of the waves as they wash against the shore, and the calls of birds in the distance. Allow yourself to relax and enjoy the beach for several minutes.*

Meditative practices, including centering and chanting, have proven to be very useful techniques in promoting relaxation. If you are experienced or interested in meditation, we encourage you to pursue this practice. Research has demonstrated that individuals who meditate regularly can reduce a variety of stress-related difficulties including high blood pressure, anxiety, panic, and insomnia.[5]

Many individuals find that music provides an easy way to create a feeling of relaxation or relief. Studies show that music reduces anxiety. You may already know that specific types of music have a relaxing effect on you. You can use music deliberately in order to create a rather immediate change in your stress level.

Other people have found that certain types of gentle, focused movement can reduce stress, anxiety, and muscle tension. Using dance or Tai Chi, a form of moving meditation, can be effective in reducing stress and calming the sympathetic nervous system. Some of us have nervous systems that relax better after movement of some kind, and if that works for you, make sure you deliberately use movement-based methods of relaxation.

Finally, evidence suggests that our pets can be useful sources of relaxation, too. Research clearly documents that spending time petting a dog or cat has a soothing effect. For example, individuals who took a stress test in their home experienced significantly less nervous system reactivity (e.g., racing pulse) when they were tested in the presence of a pet dog rather than a friend. This suggests that pets have a buffering effect on sympathetic nervous system activation.[6] Many people who have pets will acknowledge that their pets are helpful in reducing feelings of anxiety; perhaps it is because of their playfulness and nonjudgmental nature.

Relaxation You Can Use

The ability to relax is only beneficial if you can make use of it when you need it. If you are only able to achieve relaxation while lying down, or only when it is perfectly silent, you have not trained the response effectively. It is essential that you strengthen your ability to relax yourself under a variety of conditions. If you are prone to panic attacks, relaxation can be used to provide relief from the attack by lessening its symptoms.

Choose relaxation strategies that seem to have a beneficial effect on you. They can be as simple as diaphragmatic breathing or spending time with a pet. They can include music or imagery. Even engaging in massage or sexual activities can help to produce feelings of pleasure and relaxation. If an activity helps you to focus your mind on something pleasant, and to reduce muscle tension and other signs of sympathetic activation, it is promoting relaxation. The goal is to increase the activation of your parasympathetic nervous system to help you recover from the stress response and to promote well-being.

How Often Should I Practice Relaxation?

Relaxation techniques should be practiced regularly each day. You should make a habit of including relaxation in your daily schedule. Consider practicing during the breaks you take at work, or as you travel from one location to another. Look for other opportunities in your day to take a couple of minutes to relax. Try to schedule at least three or four opportunities to relax each day. Even a five-minute relaxation session can reduce your heart rate and muscle tension. And do not always wait until the end of the day to relax - schedule times in the morning to relax, too. Think of these as periods during which you "reset" your body, interrupting sympathetic nervous system activation and turning on your parasympathetic nervous system.

Those of us struggling with anxiety know that tension can gradually build during the day. By the end of the day, we find our muscles - particularly in our back and neck - have become tense and sore. If you repeatedly catch muscle tension as it builds up during the day and relax those muscles, you can correct your level of body tension so that it does not result in stiffness and pain.

Repeated, brief relaxation exercises are an essential part of coping with anxiety. Your amygdala is likely to keep turning on your sympathetic nervous system during the day. You need to keep turning it back off by using relaxation to activate the parasympathetic system. If you practice relaxation techniques enough, eventually they will become second nature and will help to curb your anxiety.

As you can see, there are many approaches to relaxation that can be helpful in reducing anxiety and stress. The point is that there is no "right" way to achieve relaxation; you simply need to find what techniques work best for you. Whatever approach you choose, incorporating regular opportunities for relaxation into your daily schedule is an essential part of coping with fear and anxiety. Not only does it lower your overall stress level, but relaxation techniques also can come in handy in particularly anxious situations.

Why Fight It? Using Exercise to Cope with Anxiety

The Freeze/Fight/Flight response has been programmed into our bodies through evolution. Perhaps, instead of fighting this ancient response, we should work *with* it at times. If your sympathetic nervous system is activated, as it often is for those who suffer from anxiety, perhaps you should put it to use, as nature intended. In other words, perhaps you should not resist the urge to fight or flee – instead, we can work with that drive and utilize those muscles.

A regular exercise program has been shown to reduce sympathetic nervous system activity,[7] a beneficial adjustment for all anxiety sufferers. **Exercise** is a very effective way to reduce muscle tension by making use of the blood flow directed to your extremities by the activated sympathetic nervous system. When you run, or even walk, you are making use of muscles that have been prepared for action. After you exercise, the muscle relaxation that follows is substantial and relatively long-lasting. Examining some of the effects of exercise on the body and on the brain can clarify why exercise is a useful strategy in coping with anxiety.

<u>*Consider This:*</u>

How often do you exercise each week? How long does each period of exercise last? Do you feel less anxious after exercise?

Exercise's Effects on the Body

There are a variety of types of exercise, including flexibility training, weight training, and aerobic workouts. The type of exercises that are most consistent with the reactions of the sympathetic nervous system are **aerobic exercises**, which make use of large muscle groups in rhythmic movements at a moderate level of intensity. Common aerobic exercises include running, walking, cycling, swimming, and even dancing.

The benefits of exercise for the body are great. Not only does regular exercise increase muscle tone and fitness, but it also can reduce excess weight. Regular aerobic exercise strengthens the functioning of the heart and lungs, and reduces the resting heart rate, contributing to an overall improvement in cardiovascular health. Aerobic exercise also tends to increase an individual's metabolic rate and energy level. It has the additional beneficial effect of improving mood. High impact aerobics can even stimulate bone growth and reduce the risk of osteoporosis. So, if you use exercise to help you cope with anxiety, you are getting a windfall of extra benefits, as well.

Risks of exercise are also apparent, and some forms of exercise, such as jogging, are high impact activities that can lead to a variety of injuries. Before you attempt any exercise routine, you should consider your fitness level and the chance of injuries. Especially if you have been relatively inactive, you should consult your physician before undertaking any new exercise program. Nevertheless, you should not let a lack of experience discourage you, because almost anyone can engage in exercises such as walking without much difficulty or risk.

<u>Consider This</u>:

If you do not regularly exercise, would you consider beginning an exercise program to decrease the sympathetic nervous system

*activation that anxiety creates? Which type
of exercise most appeals to you?*

Exercise and Anxiety

We recommend exercise because, a variety of
studies have demonstrated that aerobic exercise not
only benefits our bodies, but also reduces anxiety.[8]
Even after only twenty minutes of exercise, a reduction
in anxiety can be measured. This reduction in anxiety
is greatest for individuals who have higher levels of
anxiety to begin with,[9] suggesting that the benefits of
exercise are most pronounced for those who are coping
with high levels of anxiety. Note that one study found
that 40 minutes of exercise (including a warm up and
cool down period) was as effective as 30 minutes of
relaxation in reducing anxiety caused by distressing
images.[10] Also, individuals who used relaxation or
aerobic exercise experienced greater anxiety reduction
than did individuals in a control group who did nothing
to cope with their distress.

How long does the feeling of relief created by
exercise last? Generally, muscle tension is relaxed for
at least an hour and a half, and the reduction in anxiety
lasts from four to six hours.[11] If you consider that 20
minutes of sustained exercise may result in hours of
relief from tension and anxiety, the benefits are clear.
A carefully timed exercise routine may allow you to
reduce your anxiety level at a period of the day when
you anticipate that it may be increasing. You may be
able to obtain a tranquilizing effect without taking
tranquilizers.

Furthermore, the benefits of exercise are not only short-term. Research shows that after weeks of regular exercise, a person's general level of anxiety is reduced.[12] This means that exercise not only reduces anxiety on the day that you exercise, but that a routine program of exercise has the additional effect of reducing a person's overall level of anxiety. A person who exercises for at least ten weeks becomes less anxious, in general.[13]

Effects of Exercise on the Brain

The finding that exercise reduces anxiety has led researchers to try to discover what is happening in the brain that underlies this process. Many people are familiar with the experience of a "runner's high" in which a person who is running feels a sense of euphoria after crossing a certain threshold of exertion. Aerobic workouts have been shown to cause neurotransmitters called **endorphins** to be released into the bloodstream, and these neurotransmitters have been proposed to be the cause of this feeling of exhilaration.[14] Endorphin is the short name for "endogenous morphine" (meaning "natural morphine") and, as the name suggests, this neurotransmitter is a morphine-like compound that can reduce pain and produce a sense of well-being through its effects in the brain.

Consider This:

Have you ever found yourself feeling very pleasant emotions after exercising? Have

*you ever experienced anything that you
would describe as natural euphoria?*

In studies of humans, the blood concentrations of
endorphins have been shown to increase during
exercise and to correlate with feelings of euphoria.
Unfortunately, we know that endorphins in the blood
stream do not cross the blood-brain barrier to enter the
brain directly. This means that studies of blood levels
of endorphins in people do not tell us exactly what is
going on in their brains; we must turn to animal studies
to answer this question.

When laboratory rats are offered free access to a
running wheel, they generally make use of it. What's
more, the level of endorphins in their brains increases,
and remains high for 24 to 48 hours, only returning to
normal levels after 96 hours.[15] This finding indicates,
once again, that exercise's effects on the brain last
longer than the exercise period itself, and may in fact
be maintained for days. Taking it a step further, these
studies suggest that humans, too, have ways to change
their brain chemistry. When we exercise, not only are
we raising the amount of endorphins for that day, but
probably for days afterward.

Additional research involving rats running on their
wheels has shown that other brain chemicals are
altered by exercise, too. Increases have been shown in
the neurotransmitters serotonin,[16] dopamine, and
norepinephrine.[17] Even more surprising to scientists is
that the brain itself can change; wheel running in rats is
associated with the development of new cells in the
hippocampus.[18] Twenty years ago, new cell growth in
the brain was not even considered possible. Now we

know that one can increase levels of neurotransmitters and promote the growth of new cells in the brain without taking medications – thus avoiding their high costs and unpleasant side effects.

Studies of the electrical activity in the brain while people are exercising indicate that exercise tends to modify which areas of the brain are stimulated. After running on a treadmill for 30 minutes, for example, men showed greater activation in the left frontal area compared to the right frontal area.[19] Greater activation in the left frontal area has been associated with positive moods, whereas greater left frontal activation has been linked to depression. Once again, we find evidence that exercise may stimulate the brain in a manner that produces a more optimistic mindset; such positive feelings are likely to help reduce anxiety.

Some have suggested that exercise's beneficial effects are due to the increased sense of control that it gives an individual. When an individual sees and feels the positive results of exercise, he or she may experience a feeling of mastery or accomplishment that provides a sense of encouragement. Others suggest that exercise is beneficial as a distraction from thoughts or feelings that are distressing. Whatever the reason for the beneficial effects of exercise, it seems clear that we should take these effects seriously. So, when looking for a way to increase your level of relaxation and to improve your mood, consider exercise one of your most promising options.

Onward

Not only do diaphragmatic breathing, relaxation and exercise lower one's stress level in general, but you should realize that they will be very helpful skills to use during exposure experiences. Practice these tools so that they can assist you in reducing your heightened anxiety to more manageable levels. As we return to a discussion of exposure, remember that these resources are available to you when the going gets tough.

Chapter 8
Know Yourself and Your Triggers

The Amygdala Knows: Do You?

The most powerful tool that you have in coping with your anxiety is an in-depth understanding of your own personal anxiety responses. In order to be effective in retraining your brain to resist anxiety responses, specific knowledge about exactly what triggers your own anxiety is essential. For this reason, it is crucial that you take a close look at what situations and events are connected with your anxiety, in order to identify the triggers that should be addressed through exposure therapy.

Recall from Chapter 3 that the language of the amygdala is based on **association** and **temporal relationships** - events occurring one after another in time. As a result of our past experiences, our amygdalas have learned to associate certain situations or events with fear reactions. We are not always aware of the exact triggers that have become associated with fear, and the triggers are not necessarily "logical" ones, but the amygdala is very responsive to these triggers. In order to effectively reduce our anxiety responses, we need to identify the triggers that provoke our anxiety.

Stop for a moment and consider the variety of situations in which you experience anxiety. This may include a large number of situations, if you are thorough. Don't be discouraged. Take time to consider the big picture. Even though you may think that the process of examining so many situations can be overwhelming, you will find that hidden within the variety of situations are common triggers. For example, you may identify a large number of situations at work that trigger your anxiety, but on closer examination, a *common factor* in the different situations may appear. The same trigger may occur in different situations. Perhaps it is the presence of your boss, people raising their voices, or the need for you to engage in public speaking. In order to identify common factors, it is useful to try to consider all of the situations in which you feel troublesome anxiety.

When you consider situations in which you experience anxiety, do not forget to consider the **internal sensations** that you may react to. For example, if feeling dizzy or the experience of having to use the bathroom causes you to feel panicky, include those in your list. You may need to expose yourself to these sensations. Internal sensations can be triggers for anxiety, also.

Create an Anxiety-Provoking Situations Worksheet by making a list of situations in which you commonly experience anxiety. Use the Anxiety-Provoking Situations Worksheet example on the next page as a model. Indicate the level of anxiety that you typically feel in a given situation on a scale of 1 to 100, with 1 being minimal anxiety, 50 being moderate anxiety, and 100 being an intolerable level of anxiety. Also, indicate how often you have to deal with the situation.

For each situation, identify some of the cues that specifically elicit anxiety. Try to pinpoint the sounds you hear, what you see, the sensations you feel, and what you smell or taste. You should also consider what you think or imagine. Remember that the amygdala does not always process sensations in the detailed way that you are capable of experiencing them, so a general description of cues is sufficient. After creating the list, note whether specific cues appear repeatedly in different situations. This will help you identify your own personal triggers for anxiety.

Anxiety-Provoking Situations Worksheet

Situation that elicits anxiety	Level of Anxiety (1 low – 100 high)	Frequency (daily, once/week, once/month, etc.)	Cues/Triggers in the Situation
Neighbor's dog	70	1/week	Barking, size of dog, teeth, quick movements, jumping, thinking dog will bite me, sound of tags
Flying	100	1/month	Packing, driving to airport, imagining crash, walking in terminal, music playing, waiting at gate, boarding, fabric of seats, taking off, turbulence, landing

Sometimes the reason why a specific cue or trigger provokes anxiety is obvious. It would be clear why the sight of an elevator would elicit anxiety from someone with claustrophobia, for example. At other times, the connection between the trigger and anxiety is less clear, as with the Vietnam veteran who determined that his anxiety was due to the soap that he had used during his combat deployment. The amygdala had clearly made an association between the smell of the soap and the danger of combat. As you can see, this is not necessarily a logical association, but you can recognize where the association was made. In some cases, it may simply remain unclear why a specific cue triggers anxiety.

Remember, however, that it is not necessary to know how the cue became associated with fearful responding, because we know how to retrain the brain: we *activate* in order to *generate* new connections. Exposure to the cue and activation of fear circuitry - in the absence of a negative event - will weaken the anxiety response. Take comfort in the knowledge that we do not need to know how the response was learned in order to extinguish it.

As you create your own worksheet and identify your own specific triggers for anxiety, you may find yourself experiencing noticeable levels of stress while just thinking about the triggers. As we noted before, the amygdala reacts to triggers in a rather broad way. Once the sound of one dog growling elicits fear, the sound of other growling dogs also elicits fear, due to **generalization**. In addition, a sound that is similar to a growl can also result in a feeling of fear. Even imagining the sound of a dog growling is enough to activate the amygdala for some people.

As you review situations, do not allow any anxiety you may feel to discourage you. Instead, use your emotional responses to the cues you imagine as *indicators;* they can help you to identify what aspects of the triggers produce anxiety. In this way, you can determine more precisely what your amygdala responds to.

If, while considering these triggers, you experience some distress, don't become too concerned. It is helpful to remember that simply thinking about the fear-eliciting cues and staying calm is the first step in activating the important neural connections and beginning to retrain your amygdala. So if you begin to feel anxious, remind yourself that you are already heating up the circuits that you need to modify. Take a deep breath and stick with it!

Where to Begin?

At this point, we would like to emphasize that ridding yourself of *all* your fears is not necessary. For some individuals, the fear of flying on an airplane severely limits their careers, but others can quite easily avoid air travel their whole lives with little consequence. *If you choose to modify anxiety reactions in the situations that interfere with your ability to live your life in the way you desire, you will be on the right track.* Prioritize what situations you will focus on first by identifying the situations that most frequently or most severely limit your ability to accomplish your daily goals.

Consider This:

Contrary to what you might expect, reducing the anxiety you feel is not the central goal of this book. The central goal is to give you the power to live your life in the manner you wish, in order that you can fulfill your own aspirations. We want to give you the ability to live your life without being constantly limited by your anxiety. Therefore, when deciding what anxiety responses you wish to modify, it is essential that this process is informed by a careful consideration of your personal goals and hopes in your life.

What long-term and short-term goals do you have for yourself? Complete the following sentences, identifying specific goals. Try to imagine what you would like to do if anxiety were not a limiting factor.

In the future, I would like to see myself...
In one year, I would like to...
In eight weeks, I would like to...

After having identified your personal goals, look them over and consider which of the situations on the Anxiety-Provoking Situations Worksheet are most limiting to you in your desire to attain your goals. One woman avoided any situation involving public speaking, until she enrolled in a nursing program that required her to take a course in public speaking. Suddenly it was apparent that her anxiety about public speaking was standing in the way of her goal. This motivated her to seek assistance in reducing her public-speaking anxiety, something that she had lived with for years. We want to encourage you to focus your efforts on modifying anxiety in those situations that are blocking your own goals. Our intention is to make your goals, not your anxiety, the driving force in your life.

Identify the situations you listed on the Anxiety-Provoking Situations Worksheet that are preventing you from achieving either short- or long-term goals. Some situations will stand out as clearly interfering with your life. After you have identified a variety of these situations, you can decide where to begin in the process of reducing your anxiety through exposure.

How do you select which situation to focus on first? You may start by considering which situations you are dealing with most frequently. These may be the situations that you choose to focus on immediately. Or, you may choose to consider which situations result in the highest levels of anxiety and choose to modify those anxiety reactions first. In any case, it is essential to prioritize your exposure plan by choosing to focus on situations in which anxiety reduction will make a *real difference* in your life.

Select one situation from your worksheet to begin. Start by reviewing the anxiety-producing triggers that are a part of this situation. Prepare yourself to activate the circuits in your brain that are storing information about these triggers, in order to generate new connections that will allow you to extinguish your anxiety responses. Keeping these triggers in mind, look back over Chapter 3 to remind yourself of the language of the amygdala. Use the diagrams to help you see what triggers are connected with fear and anxiety. Review Chapters 5 and 6 to identify strategies that will make exposure most effective. Considering such factors as context and safety signals will increase your likelihood of success.

Once you and your doctor or therapist have selected the situation that you want to focus on, you will need to decide whether you want to use the gentler approach of systematic desensitization or if you want to plunge right in with flooding. In the systematic desensitization approach, you take the process step by step in a gradual way; it will take some time to work your way to the most challenging situations. Using flooding, you plunge right into some of the most challenging situations and work through them in an intense process. Flooding is quicker, but either approach will work. We will help you to break down the process into a hierarchy of steps, but you can approach the process as intensely as you feel comfortable.

Now you are ready to begin extinguishing the anxiety associated with the situation you would like to focus on first. (Other situations can be identified as ones you will work on in the future, and ones that you need not trouble yourself to change.) Select the situation that you wish to begin with, and work with your therapist to create a hierarchy based upon this situation.

Creating a Hierarchy for Exposure

A **hierarchy** is an ordered list of steps that you will use in exposure therapy. Examine one specific anxiety-provoking situation, and make a hierarchy that begins with the behaviors that are least anxiety provoking. The list eventually will progress to behaviors that require exposure to triggers that produce the most anxiety.

Let's use the example of a woman who has difficulty shopping in a mall. We would ask the woman to identify the *most stressful* behavior that could be required of her. Perhaps she would respond: "Going into a crowded store and standing in line until I make a purchase." On the other hand, she could be asked to identify a behavior that would elicit *some* anxiety, but which she is fairly confident that she would be able to carry out. She may respond: "I could drive to the parking lot and find a parking space." Once we have these anchoring points, one representing extreme anxiety, and the other representing minimal anxiety, we have the beginning of a hierarchy. Now we ask our anxious shopper to tell us at least five more behaviors, from the least anxiety provoking to the most anxiety provoking, which would fall in between these two anchoring points.

When creating a hierarchy, the level of anxiety increases with each step because of the increasing demands added with each task. Sometimes what varies is what is expected of the person. For example, it might provoke more anxiety to be required to purchase something than to simply walk around in the mall. In other cases, the nature of the cues in the situation changes, such as whether the mall is very crowded during peak shopping times, or relatively empty during a weekday morning. Other aspects of the situation that may change could include whether a supportive person is present, or whether you are alone. In any case, your own hierarchy steps are constructed by considering what reaction you will have to the specific situation in each step.

Focus on Your Own Reactions and Goals

Different individuals will construct different hierarchies for themselves. Your goal is to construct a hierarchy that reflects your own levels of anxiety, with increasing levels of anxiety at each step. The correct order of steps is not necessarily a logical one: it is based on your reactions to the situations. For some people, entering a mall alone is more anxiety provoking than standing in line for a purchase, and for others the opposite might be the case.

Our anxious shopper is asked to break down her shopping experience into steps, and she produces this list:

- *Driving to the parking lot; finding a place*
- *Walking from the car to the mall*
- *Walking around the mall with a supportive friend*
- *Walking around the mall alone*
- *Walking around the mall alone when it is crowded*
- *Being in a crowded store*
- *Selecting an item to purchase*
- *Thinking about purchasing it*
- *Asking a clerk a question about some item*
- *Standing in line until I make a purchase*
- *Walking back to the car after being in mall*

Construct your own hierarchy in a specific situation using the Hierarchy Template below. Rate each step according to the level of anxiety it produces (1-100). The first step in the hierarchy is the *least* anxiety-provoking one (with the lowest numerical anxiety level). The steps should be ordered from the lowest anxiety level to the highest. If you are trying to use a gradual approach, and you note a particularly large "jump" in anxiety level from one step to the next (from 30 to 70, for example), you may want to insert an intermediate step between those two tasks, so that the increase in anxiety from step to step is a gradual one. If you are more willing to use a flooding approach, increases in anxiety like this may be acceptable to you.

Hierarchy Template

Step Number	Description of Behavior/ Situation in Step	Level of Anxiety (1-100)
1		
2		
3		
4		
5		
6		
7		
8		

The final step of the hierarchy is obviously the most anxiety-provoking one, but it should be a goal that you are attempting to reach. Make certain that your final step is indeed something that you are motivated to accomplish. Our anxious shopper may have the ultimate goal of independently purchasing a gift for her husband before their anniversary, or she may have the goal of accompanying her husband as they shop for patio furniture. It is essential that the final step should be a goal that you are interested in achieving. Your hierarchy should move you in the direction of being able to live your life in the manner you wish, without your anxiety getting in the way.

Our anxious shopper is asked to list different situations, and to rate their anxiety level, and she produces this list:

Situation	Anxiety Level
Driving to the parking lot, and finding a place.	15
Walking from the car to the mall	25
Walking around the mall with a supportive friend	20
Walking around the mall alone	30
Being in a crowded store	50
Walking around the mall alone when it is crowded	60
Selecting an item to purchase	70
Thinking about purchasing it	75
Asking a clerk a question about some item	80
Standing in line until I make a purchase	90
Walking back to the car after being in the mall	15

Using the Hierarchy in Exposure Exercises

Your hierarchy is used by you and your therapist to design your own exposure exercises. In these exercises, you will retrain your amygdala by activating specific fear circuits in order to create new connections that will help you to resist fear and anxiety. First, you put the situations you have listed in order from least anxiety provoking to most anxiety provoking.

An exposure hierarchy for our anxious shopper is illustrated below. Notice how the situations are reordered into steps in terms of increasing anxiety, and notice that there is a large increase in anxiety from Step 5 to Step 6.

Step Number	Description of Behavior/ Situation in Step	Level of Anxiety (1-100)
1	*Driving to parking lot, and finding a place.*	15
2	*Walking back to the car after being in mall.*	15
3	*Walking around the mall with a supportive friend*	20
4	*Walking from the car to the mall*	25
5	*Walking around the mall alone*	30
6	*Being in a crowded store*	50
7	*Walking around the mall alone when it is crowded.*	60
8	*Selecting an item to purchase*	70
9	*Thinking about purchasing it*	75
10	*Asking a clerk a question about some item.*	80
11	*Standing in line until I make a purchase.*	90

You will exposure yourself to each step in your hierarchy, working from lower levels of anxiety to higher levels. As you work through your hierarchy, your relaxation skills will be very useful. Breathing deeply and keeping your muscles as relaxed as possible will help. Relaxation will help reduce the impact of anxiety on your body, and keep it from developing into panic. But remember, it is *expected* that you will feel anxious during this process - that means you are activating the fear circuits you will need to generate new connections in your brain (a bypass). You must *activate* anxiety circuits to *generate* new learning.

You may choose to begin gradually by using imagery before putting yourself in the exposure situations. To begin with imagery, you *imagine* yourself in the situation described in Step 1. Keep yourself focused on picturing yourself in the situation, thinking of the sights and sounds you would experience, and keeping yourself relaxed as you do so. When you can successfully imagine each step, and stay relaxed as you do so, you are beginning to generate new connections in your amygdala. But the real learning for your amygdala will occur when you actually put yourself in each situation. You amygdala learns best from *direct experience*.

Some people skip the imagery, and start with actual exposure to each step in the hierarchy. You and your therapist should decide the approach that is best for you. Imagery may be used to build confidence. In any case, to generate new connections, the amygdala needs direct experience with a situation. Ultimately, the goal is for you to accomplish each step in the hierarchy, and to stay in each situation until your fear goes down.

What to Do

Begin with Step 1. When you feel your anxiety rising, remain in the situation and breathe. Anxiety does not have to be experienced at a high level for rewiring of the circuits to occur, but if anxiety is high during exposure, this can sometimes produce faster change.[1] Remind yourself that, though uncomfortable, your anxiety during exposure is not all bad - you want to feel some anxiety because it means you are heating up the fear circuitry in preparation for change.

If you are comfortable with the flooding approach, you may choose to push yourself into pretty intense reactions. Just remember to stay in each situation until your anxiety decreases. You may require the assistance of a professional if you use flooding, to make sure that you do not escape the situation and make your anxiety worse. *For exposure to work, it is essential that you do not leave the situation until your anxiety has decreased.*

A useful guideline is to remain in the situation until you *reduce your anxiety by half.* For example, if you started at level 80, getting to level 40 would be cutting your anxiety in half. This is a sign that your amygdala is getting the message. When anxiety is reduced like this, you are beginning to make a new pathway in your brain.

Carefully monitor your thoughts during each step so that you are not increasing your anxiety by engaging in self-defeating or anxiety-provoking thoughts.

Thinking "I'm going to panic!" or "The dog is going to jump on me" does not help. Also, stay focused on the step that you are in, and do not anticipate other tasks that you have yet to face. Take one step at a time. Some useful coping thoughts are identified below.

Useful Coping Thoughts for Exposure

- I expect my fear to rise, but I can manage it.

- Stay focused on this situation. This is all I have to manage right now.

- Keep breathing, this won't last long.

- Relax my muscles. Let the tension go.

- I'm activating my fear circuits to change them. I'm taking control.

- Just stay until the fear decreases. It will decrease if I wait.

- I must activate to generate.

Repeat these procedures for each step in the hierarchy until you can complete each step with confidence and little anxiety. *Exposure to each step must be done repeatedly for change to occur in your amygdala.* Remember to breathe and to use relaxation techniques to cope with the anxiety you feel during these exercises. Each repetition of a step should be easier than the last. Make sure you plan in advance to give yourself opportunities for these exposures. If you don't schedule and repeat them, you will not experience change in your brain and your fears and anxiety will remain unaltered. The more that you are limited by your anxiety, the more frequently you need to practice the exposure exercises in order to regain control of your life.

When you find that you can complete Step 1 with confidence, move on to Step 2. As you proceed, you will find that, as the steps increase, it may take longer for exposure to result in a decrease in anxiety. This is because each step is placing you in a situation that provokes more anxiety. It also means you are making progress! Just stay in each situation until you have successfully reduced anxiety, and repeat the process until you feel comfortable enough to stay calm in the situation.

Do not forget to reward yourself for your progress at each step. You deserve a reward for putting yourself through these difficult exercises in order to retrain your amygdala. Think of ways to treat yourself to something special in order to congratulate yourself for your efforts. The reward may be as small as an ice cream cone, or a phone call to brag to a supportive friend. We also see nothing wrong with promising yourself a large or expensive reward when you accomplish your exposure hierarchy—as long as you can afford it! These rewards acknowledge the effort that you are putting into the processes of educating your amygdala.

Remember, exposure is a "no pain, no gain" proposition, but success is extremely worthwhile!

What Not to Do

During each step of the hierarchy, there are some important points that you should keep in mind. One essential thing to remember is to try not to leave the situation while your fear is still high. When you escape - and feel relief after escaping - you teach your brain that escape is the answer. This will only increase your anxiety in the future as your amygdala tries to compel you into escaping again. Resist the urge to escape. Stay in control of your behavior. Do not let the anxiety take control of you.

You should also **avoid** safety-seeking behaviors like those listed below:

- Having extra medicine available so that you can use it in an emergency

- Having a safe person present for all of your steps

- Carrying lucky charms of various kinds

- Holding on to objects

- Wearing sunglasses

- Sitting in a particular position or location

- Talking on a cell phone

- Staying near an exit or a bathroom

As noted in Chapter 6, these behaviors can undermine the effectiveness of all your hard work during the exposure exercises. When safety-seeking behaviors are used, exposure is only partial and it does not result in the changes in the brain that we are seeking. If you do use a safety-seeking behavior during some of your steps, make sure you eliminate it in later steps. Carefully eliminating these safety behaviors will make sure that your hard work during exposure is having the desired effect.

Finally, during exposure, you should avoid thinking thoughts that will increase your fear. Keep your focus on what is right in front of you, not on what might happen. We are all capable of making the situation worse by thinking negative thoughts. So take care not to **catastrophize** or to magnify the problem with your thoughts.

Persevere!

Exposure is not easy. If possible, find a therapist who provides exposure therapy to help you with the process. In addition to working through a hierarchy, therapists may incorporate different exercises into treatment to desensitize you to the physical sensations resulting from anxiety (i.e., heart palpitation, shallow breathing, lightheadedness). These approaches might include **biofeedback** or **interoceptive exposure.** Biofeedback attempts to help you gain mental control over body processes using observable signals (e.g. learning to slow your heart rate while watching it on a monitor). Interoceptive exposure uses simulations (i.e., exercise, intentional hyperventilation, breathing through a straw, spinning in a chair) in an attempt to make a person more accustomed to the physical symptoms one experiences when anxious. Don't forget that internal cues should be included in your exposure hierarchy. Learning to manage unpleasant sensations will help to lessen anxiety during exposure exercises.

The most important element of exposure therapy is practice, practice, practice. The only way the amygdala learns is through experience. It is going to be upsetting, even daunting at times. There will be times when you feel too busy, and times when you feel too scared. But, if you *really* want to overcome your anxiety, you need to do the hard work. Just like having toned abdominal muscles requires doing a lot of sit-ups, extinguishing fear entails facing the situation and conquering it one step at a time. Building the bypass and traveling it often is the best means of achieving lasting relief from anxiety. Your amygdala can and will change if you are willing to put the time, effort, and courage into challenging your fears and teaching your amygdala an alternative response.

Chapter 9
Brain Medicine

The Role of Medications

Now that you have an understanding of some of the processes in the brain that underlie or influence the experience of anxiety, we can examine how medications and other drugs affect these processes. Learning to resist fear is an active process, not a passive one that can be accomplished solely by taking medications to erase fear; it does not work that way. Medications help us to cope, especially in the short term. Medications also give us an opportunity to teach the brain to extinguish anxiety over the long term, especially when they allow us to seek and tolerate exposure experiences. No medication has been designed that will rewire a circuit or form new connections in the absence of *experience*. But the good news is that we are learning more about how the circuitry in the brain can be trained to resist fear and anxiety, with and without medication.

An essential point to keep in mind is that the brain is a living, changing organ which has the potential to modify and rewire itself with each new event that we experience. Yes, the substances we introduce into the brain can change its structure and functioning, but so can each encounter that we have with our fears. Research on the brain has demonstrated how essential our experiences are to the process of shaping brain circuitry in the amygdala. The amygdala needs *experience* to learn.

As we discussed in Chapter 5, it is not easy to seek out exposure experiences that will train our brain to resist anxiety. Anxieties and fears often cause us to limit our experiences. Fears can shrink our world down to narrow confines. We avoid places; we don't challenge ourselves; we restrict our interpersonal activities. Avoidance prevents us from providing the brain with opportunities to learn how to resist the old patterns of fear-based responding. The brain's typical pattern of functioning creates avoidance that only serves to preserve the state that the brain is in. The brain becomes stuck in these patterns, and life becomes a fear-perpetuating vicious circle.

Medication may be necessary to help some individuals to interrupt this vicious circle. Overcoming certain anxiety disorders, such as phobias, usually does not require medication, because phobias appear to be less limiting and can be treated successfully in psychotherapy. For other anxiety disorders, individuals may require medication temporarily or for the rest of their lives due to the disorder's pervasiveness. *Our goal is to help you to identify ways to use medication in the process of training your brain to resist, ignore, or modify anxiety responses.*

Medication can be helpful, but always remember that, by itself, medication will not provide you with the learning experiences that allow your brain to build bypass routes and extinguish fear. In fact, some medications, while reducing anxiety, may interfere with the brain's ability to learn (or rewire itself) to resist anxiety. For this reason, we will identify not only the short-term effects of each medication on reducing anxiety, but also the way each medication affects the rewiring of anxiety-related circuitry in the brain - because rewiring this circuitry is what accomplishes lasting change.

Weigh the Pros and Cons with Your Doctor

A variety of medications have been found to be helpful in treating anxiety disorders, but none of the medications are seen as ideal for every patient. While the Selective Serotonin Reuptake Inhibitors (SSRIs) are often considered to have the most advantages and fewest disadvantages, each individual needs to work with his or her physician to identify the best approach. This book is not intended to replace appropriate medical treatment, and cannot substitute for the advice of physicians and therapists who are familiar with your situation. This chapter is intended to identify relevant information that you should discuss with your treatment providers.

An important issue you should consider is whether you are using medication for long-term change or short-term relief. Evidence[1] suggests that medications that are effective in suppressing anxiety often must be continued for long periods of time to maintain their results. When medication use is discontinued, problems with anxiety frequently return. In fact, in some cases, especially with the use of benzodiazepines, anxiety problems may actually worsen when the medication is discontinued. In contrast, you are learning that some types of therapy, especially

Cognitive Behavioral Therapy utilizing exposure, sustain their positive effects even after formal therapy sessions are completed.

Speaking of therapy, the effect of medication on one's progress in therapy should be considered. Some medications have been shown to increase or decrease the effectiveness of various therapeutic approaches, so we will address these findings when we discuss specific approaches such as exposure and cognitive techniques. Often a combination of approaches, with different treatment phases, is best. Be sure to discuss this information with your doctor to ensure that your treatment plan is helping you to achieve the most beneficial outcome.

Consider This:

Review the medications you have taken to treat your anxiety, and identify what category each medication belongs to (Benzodiazepine, SSRI, Beta Blocker, etc.) You may need to consult www.RxList.com or www.MedlinePlus.gov for information. What has been the impact of each medication? Consider positive and negative effects, including side effects. Use a table like the one below.

Medication	Category	Positive Effects	Negative Effects

Do We Know How Medications Affect the Brain?

Obviously, medication is most effective when the medication's effects are understood - and the medicine is used strategically. What you have learned about how anxiety is created in the brain, and what you know about the way specific experiences can rewire fear circuitry is powerful knowledge. Our goal in this book is to assist you in designing experiences that will allow you to train your brain to resist fear and anxiety. As a result of reading this chapter, you will become better informed about how medications can enhance, complement, or interfere with this learning process.

While we will do our best to explain the effects of specific medications, at this time, we must make a rather significant confession: no one knows for sure how some of the medications exert their effects on the brain. One only has to read the *Physician's Desk Reference* (*PDR*) to validate this surprising state of affairs. Just look up references to medications taken to treat anxiety and count how many times a statement such as "Their exact mechanism of action is unknown"[2] is made.

Research is underway to identify exactly how certain medications affect brain processes, but in some cases we really cannot be certain at this time. As we discuss each type of medication, we will make use of the most current information. Still, we must admit that a surprising number of medications are prescribed for the effects they produce on anxiety, despite the fact that we don't know exactly why or how they work. (By the way, do not assume that this state of affairs is only characteristic of medication for anxiety. The process through which aspirin - salicylic acid - achieves its effects was only identified in the 1970s, despite its use for centuries.)

Finally, we must note a common limitation in the research on medications used to treat chronic conditions. Studies that examine the long-term effects of medications on the brain are few and far between. Most drugs approved for the treatment of anxiety disorders are approved on the basis of their short-term effects. Little empirical information exists about the long-term effects of many medications, since such trials are costly. Despite the fact that medications are often prescribed for decades, modest evidence exists about how taking some medications affects the brain after long-term use.

Consider This:

Make a list of the medications that you are currently taking. How long have you been taking each medication? Has the dosage changed during the period you have been taking each medication? If so, has it increased or decreased?

In summary, our knowledge of how medications affect the process of anxiety is limited, although it is increasing with every new study. We need to attend to information about short-term and long-term effects of medications, and recognize the limits of our knowledge. Just because a medication has some short-term positive effects does not mean that we have found the cause of the underlying problem.

Another aspirin analogy[3] may help to illustrate the potential problem. Imagine that you cracked a tooth on some hard candy, and developed an abscess in the tooth. As a result, you were experiencing a toothache and a low grade fever. If you took aspirin, and both the toothache and fever disappeared, would it be correct to assume that your difficulties were due to a shortage of aspirin in your system? Would it make sense to say that your problems were due to an "aspirin imbalance" and that regular use of aspirin would correct the problem? Obviously not! The point is that we must be cautious about how we interpret the reason for a medication's effectiveness. Both laboratory research and new brain-imaging studies are helping to shed light on what areas in the brain are affected by medications; they offer hope for clarifying the causes of anxiety and how best to respond to it.

Side Effects

No discussion of medication would be complete without addressing the ubiquitous problem of "side effects." **Side effects** are unintended adverse consequences that are associated with taking medication. In the case of anxiety-focused medications, side effects can range from stomach upset to confusion, from muscle weakness to sexual dysfunction.

Why do we have to contend with side effects when we take medications for anxiety? First, we have to recognize that our brain uses a certain set of chemicals called **neurotransmitters** that allow neurons to communicate with each other. The brain and the rest of the body use a limited number of these neurotransmitters in multiple neurological processes. Just as you probably use the same fuel (gasoline) in your minivan, snow blower, and lawnmower, the human body uses similar neurotransmitters in a variety of different systems.

Side effects result from the fact that the same neurotransmitter is used in different systems throughout the body. In the design of our nervous system, the same neurotransmitter is often used for surprisingly different purposes. For example, the same neurotransmitter (acetylcholine) is used for encoding memories and for regulating heart rate. Medications designed to influence a neurotransmitter's activity in one set of circuits may also have the "side effect" of influencing a completely unrelated process. Therefore, many medications designed to have effects on the neurotransmitters in fear circuitry may have effects in other parts of the nervous system and the body.

As an example, consider serotonin, a neurotransmitter often thought to be involved in areas of the brain that create anxiety. Medications used to target serotonin levels in the brain in the hopes of reducing anxiety may also affect our intestinal processes, because serotonin plays a key role in coordinating motility in the intestines. This results in side effects that can include constipation or diarrhea.

WARNING:
MAY CAUSE DIZZINESS

Because it is currently impossible to deliver a neurotransmitter to a specific location without influencing other parts of the nervous system, we are likely to experience side effects whenever we take medications for anxiety. When we try to affect anxiety, we may interfere with sleep patterns or sex drive, for example. Furthermore, levels of one neurotransmitter in the brain may adjust in response to changes in other neurotransmitters.[4] Therefore, it is difficult to make one isolated change in the brain without affecting other systems.

So you see, for a variety of reasons, the use of medications results in side effects - a broader range of effects than we would have anticipated - and, when you combine medications, the effects become even more complicated. Finally, because no two brains or bodies are exactly alike, medications frequently will have different effects on different people. So a medication that is helpful for one person may result in only negative effects for another person. We cannot predict the response a specific individual will have to a specific medication. Under a doctor's supervision, a person may have to try a few different medications before finding the one that works best.

It is important to note that side effects are also likely to result from the long-term use of medications (longer than one or two years). The brain is a responsive and adaptive system, and it adjusts to changes in brain chemistry in complex and sometimes unexpected ways. The brain changes its structure, or reduces its production of specific chemicals or proteins, in response to the continued presence of certain medications. Long-term effects on the brain, which are not the intended effects of treatment, can occur in response to medications - but we know very little about these effects because they are rarely studied. Pharmaceutical companies that design and evaluate medications tend to focus primarily on their short-term benefits and safety; clinical trials of the effects of medication rarely last more than one year.

Unintended short-term effects and unexpected long-term effects are both likely consequences of using medications to control anxiety. You will see specific side effects mentioned for each set of medications described below. Because each individual is unique, and because medication effects are known to vary with different ethnic, gender, and age groups, the side effects that a specific person may experience cannot be predicted with certainty. Be sure to consult with your doctor about the side effects of any medications you take or plan to take as part of your treatment.

Consider This:

If you have taken medications for your anxiety, have you experienced side effects? If so, what are some of the side effects you experienced? How problematic were side effects for you?

BENZODIAZEPINES

The **benzodiazepines**, medications such as Valium (diazepam), Xanax (alprazolam), and Klonopin (clonazepam), have calming effects and, unlike many other medications, provide immediate relief from anxiety. They are often called anxiolytics (from _anxi_ [torment] and *lytic* [to loosen]) because they are so effective at reducing anxiety. Benzodiazepines often improve a person's ability to sleep, but they are not effective in treating depression. Side effects such as sedation, nausea, or muscle weakness often occur with benzodiazepine use, and combining benzodiazepines with alcohol can be fatal. Long-term side effects of benzodiazepines may include impairment in a variety of cognitive skills, including verbal learning and memory.[5]

Benzodiazepines are addictive, which means that prolonged use of these drugs leads to physiological dependence. Increased dosages may be needed to sustain effects and symptoms of withdrawal are likely when one discontinues the medication. Symptoms of withdrawal may include insomnia, agitation, anxiety, headache, and loss of appetite. Various anxiety-like symptoms of withdrawal can lead people going through withdrawal to believe that their anxiety disorder is worsening. This is known as **rebound anxiety**. Discontinuation of the use of benzodiazepines can be successfully accomplished when a slow tapering of the medication is employed, but it should be approached cautiously, under the care of a physician. Negative effects, including seizures, are possible if withdrawal is undertaken too quickly.

How Do Benzodiazepines Affect Anxiety?

Although the precise mechanism by which many benzodiazepines affect anxiety is unknown,[6] it is thought that these drugs calm the fear response by increasing the effects that a neurotransmitter called gamma-aminobutyric acid. Gamma-aminobutyric acid, typically called GABA, inhibits the activity of neural circuits in the amygdala (and other parts of the brain). In other words, when benzodiazepines provide a GABA boost of sorts, it slows neuron activity in the amygdala and reduces anxiety. The result is that benzodiazepines reduce fear-related responses, such as defensive behaviors (escape, freezing), as well as autonomic nervous system responses (sweating, increased heart rate). The benzodiazepines probably tone down anxiety responding by inhibiting the amygdala.

Because GABA is used throughout the brain (in fact, over one third of the connections in the brain are GABA-based), the influence of benzodiazepines is not simply restricted to the brain's fear circuitry. Benzodiazepines also have an effect on general GABA transmission, thereby increasing many inhibitory processes in other neural networks. Side effects such as sedation and muscle weakness result from the inhibiting influence of GABA in these other networks.

How Do Benzodiazepines Affect Rewiring in the Fear System?

Benzodiazepines have a tranquilizing effect on the amygdala. They keep fear and anxiety in check. Unfortunately, this restraint on activation also impairs the learning process.[7] Remember that the process of extinguishing anxiety responses is based on learning new connections. Recall that you must *activate* neurons to *generate* new learning. The new learning (wiring) of extinction is *less likely* to be generated in a brain medicated with benzodiazepines. Perhaps this is why individuals who benefit most from therapy are those who are not taking benzodiazepines.[8] Because neurons must fire if they are to rewire, the impact of benzodiazepines is to slow down the process of rewiring in general. Thus, we would expect neural pathways to be less likely to be rewired when they are affected by benzodiazepines. An analogy would be to say that the amygdala can't learn well while it is sedated.

In summary, benzodiazepines act to calm the system that gives rise to the learning and experiencing of anxiety, but they also *preserve* this system as it is currently wired. Benzodiazepines probably restrict the brain's ability to create the new connections that allow alternative responses, thereby making extinction of established anxiety responses less likely. Remember "Activate to Generate?" Without activating the circuitry that stores the responses, we cannot generate new circuitry that promotes extinction learning. This suggests that if your goal is to manage anxiety, short-term benzodiazepine use can be helpful, but when attempting to extinguish anxiety, especially through exposure, benzodiazepines may interfere with the extinction process.

SSRIs - Selective Serotonin Reuptake Inhibitors

The **SSRIs**, medications such as Zoloft (sertraline), Prozac (fluoxetine), Celexa (citalopram), Lexapro (escitalopram oxalate), and Paxil (paroxetine), are most associated with the treatment of depression, but they frequently have positive effects in people suffering from anxiety. First of all, the fact that SSRIs reduce depression is beneficial for many individuals with anxiety because so often they are also dealing with depression, too. Secondly, SSRIs have been shown to reduce anxiety when prescribed for variety of anxiety disorders. Unlike benzodiazepines, however, SSRIs do not provide immediate relief; a period of one to two weeks is often required before a person notes beneficial effects. In some cases, anxiety may increase during this initial period of treatment.

Side effects associated with SSRI use include nausea, insomnia, sedation, weight gain, and sexual response difficulties. While these medications are not addictive, symptoms of withdrawal are likely when one discontinues the medication. These withdrawal symptoms have been named "**antidepressant discontinuation syndrome**" by drug companies, and they may include dizziness, sensory disturbances (tingling, for example), agitation, anxiety, and sweating. Discontinuation of the use of SSRIs should be approached gradually and cautiously under the care of a physician.

How Do SSRIs Affect Anxiety?

This class of medications is called Serotonin Reuptake Inhibitors because they block the reuptake process in neurons that utilize a neurotransmitter called serotonin. Reuptake occurs when a neuron reabsorbs the chemical it has released. When reuptake is blocked, the neurotransmitter serotonin is not reabsorbed, but is allowed to remain active longer. This increases the activity of neurons that use serotonin. We know that SSRIs exert their effects by increasing serotonin activity in the brain, but the way in which serotonin activity affects anxiety is complex and not well understood.

Which neural systems are affected by increased serotonin? Once again, side effects of the medication indicate that a variety of neural systems use serotonin as a neurotransmitter. Serotonin systems in the body regulate sleep, appetite, and digestion. Not surprisingly, the first drugs designed to affect serotonin levels often caused the side effects of drowsiness, weight gain, and nausea. Fortunately, the receptors for serotonin found in the intestines are different subtypes (5-HT3 and 5-HT4) than the receptors found in the brain (5-HT1 and 5-HT2). As the medications have been refined to better target specific serotonin receptors (and thus called *Selective* Serotonin Reuptake Inhibitors), the number of side effects has generally been reduced. Generations of SSRIs have developed, with each newly named SSRI (Prozac => Celexa => Lexapro) tending to be more "selective" in terms of the specificity of serotonin receptors affected.

So what areas in the brain are SSRIs affecting? Recent animal and human research suggests that reduction of anxiety symptoms occurs because of the way the amygdala and another brain area involved in memory, the hippocampus, are affected. [9] Exactly what is happening in these areas will probably take years to sort out completely. Only as technology advances and allows us to examine the effects on specific neurons will we truly understand what processes are being impacted.

Here is a summary of what we do know: At first it was thought that simply increasing the level of serotonin was reducing symptoms associated with anxiety and depression. This was consistent with the popular idea that depression resulted from a chemical imbalance of serotonin. But, if the increased level of serotonin itself were responsible for the change in symptoms, we would see the impact of increased serotonin immediately after a person took the medication. Instead, individuals taking SSRIs have to wait a week or more for a positive change in symptoms to occur. (In fact, some individuals may experience a worsening of anxiety symptoms at first.) It became obvious that the increase in serotonin levels itself could not be responsible for such a delayed change, so researchers began investigating other changes in neurons that could take place in 7 to 14 days, and possibly impact the symptoms of anxiety.

What is being proposed at this time is that daily use (for more than a week or two) of antidepressants eventually results in changes in the *structure* of neurons. The neurons, adapting to the new levels of serotonin, make adjustments in the number of receptors, grow new dendrites, or perhaps even promote the development of new connections or circuits.[10] In other words, the new level of serotonin may somehow stimulate the neurons to remodel themselves and their circuits in a variety of ways that are currently only partially understood. The most accurate way to characterize the change in these neurons would be to call it increased flexibility, indicating that the neurons become more capable of modification. Thus, it is theorized that SSRIs increase the brain's ability to restructure parts of itself, and that makes it more amenable to new learning.

Interestingly enough, therapists have heard descriptions of this type of experience from some of their clients long before the technology was available to detect specific changes in the neurons. Therapists reported that their clients said the use of SSRIs seemed to give them more control over what they thought - they didn't feel so "stuck" in certain thought patterns. Perhaps this is how it feels to experience increased neural flexibility. It wasn't that the medication resulted in new thoughts, but that people felt an increased flexibility in thinking that gave them the ability to create new thought patterns. For example, they were better able to change the focus of their attention or to stop dwelling on certain stimuli or thoughts. This brings us to the next question...

How Do SSRIs Affect Rewiring in the Fear System?

Research on the effects of the SSRIs has not given us clear answers about how SSRIs affect the amygdala. It is possible that the process of rewiring the fear system (i.e., building a bypass) is promoted by SSRIs. Research indicates that SSRIs promote the growth of neurons.[11] Therefore, they may make it more likely that a circuit in the brain can be modified by experience. The specific location of the rewiring and the nature of the rewiring that occurs cannot be clearly predicted at this time, however.

What is the significance of promoting the growth of neurons? A gardening analogy might prove useful at this point. Imagine that taking SSRIs is similar to using fertilizer in your garden. You are promoting new growth. You see more roots, buds, and branches. Of course, you need to be careful what you fertilize - the weeds will respond just as quickly as the roses if you are not careful. Taking care to examine which neural patterns you are strengthening would seem to be significant in making effective use of SSRI treatment. This means that it is important to consider what you are teaching your brain when you take SSRIs. Research indicates that SSRIs are most helpful in changing a person's thought processes when a person is also provided with therapy focused on modifying their thoughts.[12]

At this time, it seems reasonable to hypothesize that SSRIs have the potential to assist efforts to rewire the neural circuits underlying fear and anxiety responses. Perhaps in the near future, brain imaging research will clarify the exact effects of SSRIs on neural circuitry. Preliminary evidence[13] suggested that individuals with social phobia who took the SSRI Celexa (citalopram) showed decreased activation in the amygdala, hippocampus, and nearby cortex, but other studies have found somewhat different results.[14] At this point, we must still be cautious about asserting that SSRIs will promote rewiring in the amygdala.

BETA-BLOCKERS

Beta-blockers, medications such as Inderal (propranolol), Tenormin (atenolol), and Toprol (metoprolol), do not reduce anxiety itself, but instead reduce symptoms associated with anxiety, such as trembling or increased heart rate. Beta-blockers control these symptoms by blocking certain beta-adrenergic receptors for adrenaline. Side effects such as dizziness, breathing difficulties, cold hands or feet, tiredness, and even depression can occur with the use of beta-blockers. Side effects associated with long-term use are not well studied, but some investigations suggest that chronic use can result in impaired memory.[15]

Beta-blockers are not addictive and no long-term effects are expected when they are taken infrequently (e.g., when a beta-blocker is prescribed for a musician to take before an anxiety-provoking concert performance). Daily use of these drugs does lead to physiological dependence, however; so symptoms of withdrawal such as sweating or increased blood pressure or heart rate are likely when one discontinues the medication. Because so many of the symptoms of discontinuing beta-blockers are anxiety-like, it can lead people to believe that their anxiety disorder is worsening. The daily use of beta-blockers should not be halted abruptly, but is best accomplished through a gradual process, under the care of a physician.

How Do Beta-blockers Affect Anxiety?

You may remember our discussion in Chapter 4 of the Freeze/Fight/Flight response which occurs when the central nucleus of the amygdala turns on a variety of body systems in order to prepare a person to react to a threatening situation. The amygdala initiates these responses by activating the **autonomic nervous system**. The autonomic nervous system causes the hormone **adrenaline** to be released into the blood from the **adrenal glands** (on top of the kidneys). Adrenaline is not only a hormone - it is also a neurotransmitter that carries the message to react to stress throughout the whole body. Beta-blockers prevent or reduce specific symptoms associated with the Freeze/Fight/Flight response by "sitting" on the receptors for adrenaline, thus preventing adrenaline from activating these receptors. In this way, they "block" the effects of adrenaline. If you recall from Chapter 4, adrenaline is responsible for increased heart rate, elevated blood sugar, and dilation of arteries in the legs and arms, which prepare us for responding by running or fighting. So, beta-blockers are preventing adrenaline from shifting our bodies into this state of heightened activation.

When you take beta-blockers, you do not affect the amygdala directly; the amygdala still reacts to the situations you experience, and it still sends signals to produce adrenaline. But heart rate, trembling, and sweating are reduced because the adrenaline cannot effectively trigger these reactions. Beta-blockers do not prevent anxiety, rather, they reduce our bodies' responses.

How does this affect one's experience of anxiety? Anxious thoughts and worries are not directly reduced by beta-blockers. A person can still worry, but their physical symptoms may be lessened. If a woman tends to experience more anxiety when she notices she is sweating or her heart is pounding, however, she is less likely to experience increased anxiety if she is taking beta-blockers. Individuals with **anxiety sensitivity** who are very aware of and responsive to physical sensations may find the reduction in the symptoms of stress to be a relief.

Because receptors for adrenaline exist throughout the body, beta-blockers can affect a variety of bodily processes. Beta-blockers decrease the effects of adrenaline, reducing blood pressure, heart rate, sweating, and increasing muscle contractions in the lungs, and the uterus. Side effects are typically related to these processes, but also include nausea, headache, dizziness, insomnia and nightmares.

How Do Beta-blockers Affect Rewiring in the Fear System?

Because beta-blockers are blocking adrenaline, they do not have a direct impact on the process of rewiring the neural circuitry in the brain that creates anxiety. Fears and anxieties already wired into the amygdala are not affected, although the body's responding to them is blunted; the effects of adrenaline are hindered. There is some indication, though, that in certain cases, beta-blockers might be helpful in *preventing* fear associations from developing into anxiety-provoking memories.

Fear-related memories are especially problematic in **Post-traumatic Stress Disorder** (PTSD), where an individual keeps reliving or recalling a catastrophic event. Some evidence indicates that the reason some memories are so strong and frequently recalled is that, during a traumatic experience, adrenaline's effect on the brain is to make some memories intensified. They become "super memories." Studies are looking at ways of using beta-blockers to prevent this from occurring. For example, if adrenaline operates to enhance memories of events that evoke powerful emotions, then giving beta-blockers to a person who has just experienced a traumatic event, like a battle or a sexual assault, might prevent the person's brain from forming the type of enduring memories that often haunt survivors of these events.

Studies[16] have shown mixed results about whether Inderal (propranolol) administered after exposure to trauma reduces the symptoms of Post-traumatic Stress Disorder These results are preliminary, however, and seem to depend on the amount of beta-blocker administered and the timing of the medication. Still, this research is another example of how we can apply our knowledge of how fear is created in the brain.

BUSPAR

Buspar (buspirone) is in a class of medications called **azaspirodecanediones.** Like the SSRIs, Buspar exerts its effects by influencing the action of serotonin in the brain. In addition, it also affects **dopamine** and **norepinephrine** (also called noradrenalin), two other neurotransmitters. Buspar is less sedating than other medications used in the treatment of anxiety. Typically prescribed for the treatment of Generalized Anxiety Disorder, Buspar also tends to reduce depression, but has not been shown to be helpful in treating panic disorder. In fact, Buspar may *stimulate* central sympathetic nervous system activity. In a manner similar to the SSRIs, Buspar takes two to three weeks to produce beneficial effects. Side effects such as dizziness, headache, nausea, diarrhea, or constipation can occur. Long-term side effects of Buspar are not well studied, but to date, no indication of negative long-term effects has been found.

Individuals who previously have been treated with a benzodiazepine sometimes have a poor response to Buspar. Perhaps this is because Buspar does not have the sedating or muscle-relaxing effects of the benzodiazepines, or perhaps it is because of the delay in achieving noticeable anxiety reduction. Buspar is not addictive, and it can apparently be discontinued abruptly without negative effects; again, consult your doctor.

How Does Buspar Affect Anxiety?

Although the precise mechanism by which Buspar reduces anxiety is not completely understood, it appears that Buspar reduces the level of serotonin transmission in the brain at the same time that it contributes to an increase in dopamine and norepinephrine transmission. It is unclear why reducing serotonin transmission would influence anxiety, especially since SSRIs, which are designed to increase levels of available serotonin, also have the effect of reducing anxiety. Some researchers have looked to the effects of increasing levels of dopamine to explain Buspar's anti-anxiety properties, but no definitive explanation about the role of dopamine has been proposed.

Because anxiety reduction takes up to three weeks to occur, the effects of Buspar cannot simply be due to the changes in levels of neurotransmitters that take place within hours of the medication being administered. As with the SSRIs, it could be suggested that modifying the process of transmission somehow stimulates certain neurons to remodel themselves and their circuits in some way. Recent research indicates that Buspar may reduce anxiety through changes in neurotransmission it causes in the amygdala[17] and hippocampus.[18] The research suggests that Buspar may block the development of emotional memories, especially memories about the *context* in which a fear-eliciting event occurs.

Because serotonin and dopamine are utilized throughout the brain, Buspar influences a variety of circuitry, in addition to fear circuitry. Decreasing serotonin transmission may affect the gastrointestinal system as well as emotional processes. Increasing dopamine transmission likewise can result in a variety of effects because dopamine is involved in regulating such diverse areas as heart rate, blood pressure, thought processes, pleasure, and motivation. For this reason, side effects may include heart palpitations, depression, headaches, and nausea.

How Does Buspar Affect Rewiring in the Fear System?

If researchers are correct and Buspar does decrease the brain's ability to create emotional memories, it may have the effect of reducing the likelihood that a person will develop new fears. By interfering with the process of making emotional memories, particularly about the context in which fear occurs, Buspar may protect the brain from acquiring new fears during negative experiences. But how does Buspar affect the extinction process for already established fears? Studies to date show mixed results, so it is difficult to draw conclusions about Buspar's influence on fear circuitry at this time. In addition, most extinction research has been carried out on the effects of Buspar taken as a one-time dose, and not upon its extended use, so little useful information is available about how Buspar would affect the rewiring process.

A Note about a New Use for an Old Drug

While scientists are trying to develop new medications for the treatment of anxiety disorders, an old medication, originally developed for the treatment of tuberculosis, has shown some promise in assisting in the learning process during exposure. This medication, **D-cycloserine**, has long been approved by the Food and Drug Administration, is available in generic form, and is therefore very reasonably priced.

The use of D-cycloserine is not focused on reducing symptoms of anxiety. In fact, it doesn't appear to affect a person's experience of anxiety at all. Instead, this drug was selected for study because of its effect on neurons that are involved in the learning of extinction in the amygdala.[19] Researchers found that D-cycloserine could improve the extinction learning in rats. Interestingly, they found that D-cycloserine only helped the amygdala learn *extinction*, not fear.

It wasn't long before experiments were being conducted to determine if D-cycloserine had a similar effect in humans. Individuals who were undergoing exposure treatment were given the drug, and their results were compared to those of people who were undergoing exposure without the drug. The findings were very encouraging. People who took D-cycloserine during their exposure exercises showed significantly more improvement than those who did not take the drug.[20] It seems researchers have found a drug that facilitates the process of rewiring the circuits in the amygdala!

At this point, D-cycloserine has not been widely used, but past research on the medication (when it was used to treat tuberculosis) indicates that it has few side effects.[20] Recent studies have shown that the drug facilitates the beneficial effects of exposure in a variety of anxiety disorders, including social anxiety disorder,[21] acrophobia (fear of heights),[22] and obsessive-compulsive disorder.[23] People who took D-cycloserine before exposure sessions overcame their anxiety more quickly, with fewer exposure sessions, than did those who took placebos. Medications such as this, which work to facilitate the learning in the amygdala, are a very hopeful sign for anxiety sufferers.

Chapter 10
Cognitive Approaches:
Using the Higher Levels of the Brain

Cognitive Approaches to Anxiety

The term **cognition** is the psychological term for the mental processes that most people refer to as "thinking." Thus, cognitive approaches designed to control anxiety target our cortex-based thinking processes. Many of us have already been introduced to these cognitive approaches, either by our therapists or through reading resources that focus on how our thoughts contribute to creating anxiety.

Perhaps the best known pioneers of cognitive treatment are psychiatrist Aaron Beck and psychologist Albert Ellis.[1] Both Beck and Ellis propose that anxiety can be created or worsened by certain types of thinking. These theorists suggest that anxiety results from the way we interpret events and the possibility that we sometimes distort reality in our thinking processes. For instance, we may overemphasize the dangerousness of a situation, such as when we think about a plane crash while we are flying. Or we may interpret someone's behavior as personally relevant when it has nothing to do with ourselves, as when you assume that someone is talking during your presentation because you are boring. As a result, we may anticipate problems that never occur, or worry about bodily sensations that are, in reality, harmless. The idea is that some cognitions are illogical or unhealthy and create or exacerbate our anxiety.

Aaron Beck explains that, according to this perspective, "the individual's primary problem has to do with his construction of reality. The remedy lies in modifying the cognitive set."[2] In other words, the goal is to change the individual's way of thinking about his or her anxiety experience because this will change the person's emotional reaction to the situation. In particular, cognitive therapists focus on finding and changing thoughts that are self-defeating because they can lead to increased levels of anxiety or depression.

How does this approach to anxiety relate to the processes going on in the brain? What part of the brain are cognitive therapists focusing on? When they discuss self-defeating thoughts, cognitive therapists are primarily focused on the higher level cognitive processes that occur in the cerebral cortex. The cerebral cortex is the thinking brain - the curvy, gray-matter covered portion of our brain that fills the topmost part of our skulls.

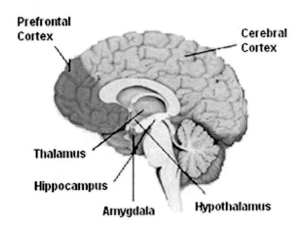

Whenever we try to change our thoughts, we are, of course, trying to modify the brain in some way. Cognitive therapists realize that changes in thinking processes are related to changes in brain functioning. Our thoughts are not simply a result of the chemical processes in our brain; they *are* the chemical processes in our brain. Thus, according to Beck, "Neurochemical changes and cognitions are the same process examined from different perspectives."[3]

As we have examined the processes in our brain that create fear and anxiety, we have discovered that anxiety can and often does occur without involving higher level thinking processes. In fact, we know from our discussions of the "express" and "local" lanes that fear reactions can be put into action *before* higher levels of cognitive processing have been completed. Does this mean that our thoughts and interpretations don't matter? No. Thoughts definitely have an impact. It is crucial to have a clear understanding of the ways in which thoughts can impact our emotional reactions as well as the ways in which they are limited in their impact. When you understand what your thoughts can and cannot do in terms of modifying anxiety, you have more ability to use your thoughts effectively in reducing your anxiety.

Can changing our thoughts prevent anxiety? Not always, because anxiety can occur automatically, without input from our higher level cognitive processing. Can our thoughts contribute to our anxiety? Absolutely. Thoughts can be an important trigger for anxiety in some cases, and in other cases, they can have the effect of increasing or decreasing our anxiety. If we change our thoughts, we may be able to interrupt or prevent our cognitive process from contributing to our anxiety.

Often, we have the potential to head-off anxiety – rather than adding fuel to the fire – by controlling what we are thinking or telling ourselves. As difficult as it may seem to change our thought processes, it is easier in many cases than changing our emotional reactions. (This is why you can find so many self-help books focused on "positive thinking" at your local bookstore.) But changing thoughts is not enough if you aren't considering the role of the amygdala, the emotional brain. If you understand the nature of the connections between your thoughts and your emotional brain, you become more effective at using your thinking brain to combat anxiety.

How the Amygdala Influences Thoughts

We noted in Chapter 3 that there are few connections from the cerebral cortex to the amygdala, but many connections from the amygdala back to the cerebral cortex. That means that while the cortex has little influence over the reactions of the amygdala, the amygdala can definitely influence the cortex, especially in terms of what becomes the focus of our thoughts and attention. This means that when the amygdala is signaling danger, it can strongly affect our thoughts.

When we become anxious, our thought processes can be impaired. If the amygdala is activating an anxiety response, it is difficult to focus our attention on anything else. We fail to see the details of our surroundings when we are merely reacting to fear. Higher level thinking processes such as what we pay attention to, what we think about, and what events we anticipate all can be influenced by the activation of the amygdala.

Unfortunately, on one level, our attempts to control our thinking processes are trumped by the activity of the amygdala. This explains why we often feel that, in many situations, our intentions and goals are overwhelmed by anxious feelings we cannot control. The ability of the cerebral cortex to interrupt the functioning of the amygdala can be fairly limited when the amygdala is strongly activated. The amygdala's responses always get priority, as though they are more responsible for our survival. We are acting on the influence of the emotional brain, not on the basis of the thinking brain.

How Thoughts Can Influence the Amygdala's Responding

While the amygdala is not directly controlled by higher cortical thought processes, it is continuously monitoring these processes. The amygdala is constantly scanning our day-to-day experiences for any indication of danger. Anxiety-related thoughts and memories are capable of making the amygdala sound the alarm, even in the absence of real danger in the external environment. Mere thoughts of anxiety-provoking situations can, by themselves, trigger an anxiety response. You don't have to directly experience something threatening to activate the amygdala - you can activate your amygdala simply by thinking about or imagining experiences that the amygdala has associated with anxiety.

Have you ever remembered a frightening event, or imagined a disaster befalling you, and found that your heart started pounding? Seemingly simple thoughts can be a powerful influence in the process of creating anxiety. Whether the amygdala receives information through the sensory route coming from the thalamus (express), or coming from our memory and conscious thought processes (local), the amygdala responds in a fairly similar way. If you have a fear of spiders, for example, and you imagine that a spider is nearby, you may find that your amygdala reacts to the imaginary spider in your thoughts and begins activating a fear response. So, too, if you have a fear of public speaking and you know you have to give a speech next week, you may begin to feel anxious today.

Just Your Imagination?

The fact that we can activate fear responses by imagining situations without actually having to be exposed to the situations we dread has long been recognized. This knowledge is what underlies the use of "imagery" in exposure therapy. Recall our explanation of systematic desensitization in Chapter 5. Often exposure therapy begins by having an individual *imagine* themselves in a situation that is feared. The amygdala will respond to their thoughts of the feared situation in much the same way as it responds to the situation itself.

In fact, you can *create* anxiety in a situation simply by worrying. Over-thinking and rehearsing negative events in your mind can form associations using the language of the amygdala. Pairings of situations and negative events can occur in your imagination, just as in real life, and have an effect on the amygdala.

For example, you may imagine yourself asking someone out on a date and being turned down, then repeat this depressing scenario over and over in your head. Eventually you create a connection between the thought of asking and the fear of rejection that is almost as strong as if the events had actually occurred. The next time you see the person, you may feel so anxious that you can barely speak! In our conditioning graphs, that situation might be diagramed like this:

Figure 10.1

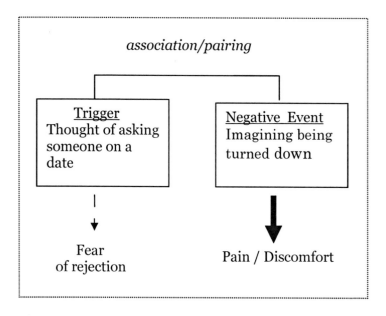

In Chapter 5, we noted that logic and reasoning should not be seen as the solution to anxiety. This is because the fear circuitry underlying anxiety is not based on logical reasoning, but on *associations* and *pairings* – the language of the amygdala. In the previous example, you are conditioning your amygdala to have an emotional reaction to this person by creating a pairing between your thoughts of that person and a negative outcome. There is no logic involved at all.

You can tell yourself over and over that your feelings are not logical, and try to fight them on these grounds. But fears and anxieties are not created or changed simply on the basis of logic in your cortex: the amygdala is involved. In order to use your thoughts to reduce your anxiety, you need to know how your thoughts impact your amygdala.

Knowing that pairings are the language of the amygdala, you can deliberately imagine *positive* outcomes to create a different emotional response by the amygdala. Imagining various positive scenarios resulting from asking this person out does not guarantee that the person will go out with you, of course, but it makes it more likely that you can keep your anxiety in check during the process. Perhaps most importantly, you can learn to recognize when your thoughts are the type that contribute to anxiety, and try to halt those thoughts before they influence your amygdala.

How to Effectively Use Thoughts to Reduce Anxiety

In order to be effective in using our thought processes to reduce anxiety, we need to recognize the kind of thoughts that are likely to create anxiety and attempt to limit these thoughts. First of all, since you are aware that you can create pairings between events just by thinking about them, you should try to be aware of times when you are doing this. If you are attempting to reduce your anxiety about driving, for example, you should avoid spending time thinking about losing control of the car, having an accident, or any other scenario that exposes you to thinking about negative situations associated with driving. Controlling your thoughts is not always easy, but if you are vigilant, it is possible.

Some of us have a strong tendency to think in ways that result in anxiety. We have a knack for coming up with negative scenarios in our heads, and are actually quite talented at imagining unlikely disastrous events. Think of your brain as cable television. Many of us get stuck watching the "**Anxiety Channel**." You have hundreds of channels on which you can focus your thinking brain, but the Anxiety Channel is, unfortunately, your favorite. Once you are aware of this tendency, you can try to modify it. In fact, it is often very helpful to think of your goal as "changing the channel."

Instead of telling yourself not to anticipate an automobile accident while you are driving, for example, you can change the channel completely by focusing your attention on a different topic. You could focus your thoughts on whatever is on the radio, or you could focus on having a conversation with someone. Being aware of your tendency to get stuck on the Anxiety Channel is a first step in using your thoughts to decrease your anxiety.

Second, there is a certain set of thoughts and beliefs that have been shown to increase anxiety and other distressing emotional responses (particularly depression). These thoughts are another good place to start your cognitive housecleaning. We call these thoughts "**Self-Defeating Thoughts.**"

On the next page, a set of Self-Defeating Thoughts is accompanied by a list of more positive "**Coping Thoughts.**" Coping Thoughts are beliefs or thoughts that are expected to have a positive effect on a person's emotional state. If you evaluate the usefulness of your thoughts by the effects that they have on you, you will see the value of coping thoughts; they are more likely to result in calm responding and an increased ability to cope with difficult situations.

Searching for Your Own Self-Defeating Thoughts

You probably recognize some Self-Defeating Thoughts in your own daily thinking. We encourage you to challenge them and to replace them with more adaptive Coping Thoughts at every possible opportunity. But the thoughts listed are only a starting point. They can give you a sense of which of your own recurrent thoughts and beliefs are self-defeating and should be challenged. Some Self-Defeating Thoughts have a whole set of "offspring" that you should be on the lookout for. Once you recognize a tendency toward a Self-Defeating Thought, you are likely to find other variations of that type of thought in many aspects of your life.

Self-Defeating Thought	Coping Thought
I must be competent and achieving at everything I undertake.	No one is perfect. I expect that I will make mistakes at times.
Everyone should like me.	No one is liked by everyone, so I am likely to encounter people who don't like me.
When things happen that I don't want to happen, it is intolerable.	When things happen that I don't want to happen, I feel upset, but I'll survive it.
It's no use trying; Things will never work out for me.	I am going to try, because if I try at least there is a chance that I will accomplish something.
The only solution is to get out of this situation.	There are many possible solutions to any problem, and I can find one.
When my heart pounds or breathing quickens, it is very dangerous, and I should worry about it.	These are typical symptoms of anxiety I have experienced many times, and they are not dangerous to me.
If I ask her out, she will say no, which will devastate me.	If I ask her out and she turns me down, it might hurt, but it won't be the end of the world.
If I fly on a plane, it could crash and I would die.	If I fly on a plane, more than likely, I'll get where I'm going safely.

Take for example the Self-Defeating Thought "I must be competent and achieving in everything I undertake." This Self-Defeating Thought has a whole brood of offspring like "I must be a good student" and "I must be the best parent." Other thoughts like "I shouldn't lose" and "I should never forget anything" are also related. These sets of beliefs add to our general anxiety level by creating an intimidating situation, when no real threat exists. If you are anxious about having guests visit your home, it could reflect the belief "I must be tidy at all times". As a result, however, you may be allowing your perfectionism to cramp your social life. Or, if you make a simple subtraction error in the books at your place of employment, and fear that you will be fired, it may emphasize your conviction that "Employees must never make mistakes" rather than reflect an actual danger of losing your job.

In general, it is useful to watch for "musts" and "shoulds" in your thinking. When you tell yourself you "should" accomplish something, or that something "should" happen according to some specific plan or schedule, you are setting yourself up for stress and worry. The term "should" makes the situation sound like a rule is being violated if events don't proceed in the specified way. Rather than saying "I should...," it is much better to say "I would like to..." That way, you aren't setting a rule to be followed, but expressing a goal or a desire.

Consider This:

Do you place demanding expectations on yourself through the use of shoulds like the following? If so, you may be able to reduce your anxiety by replacing these thoughts with Coping Thoughts.

Should Statement	Coping Thought
I should be able to keep up with this workload.	Almost anyone would struggle to keep up with a workload like this.
I should be making more money at my age.	While I would like to make more money, I am making enough to live on.
I shouldn't have to deal with difficult people or situations.	I don't enjoy dealing with difficult people or situations, but these things happen, and I'll survive the experience.

The use of the word "should" is often connected to the belief that life "should be" a certain way. Usually, it is related to the belief that life should be fair. We all know, logically, that life is not fair, but for some reason we hold on to the Self-Defeating Belief that it should be. While we can live our lives in order to create as much fairness for ourselves and others as possible, the truth is that bad things happen to good people, and evil, conniving people often escape punishment completely. Sometimes disaster strikes at the worst time, and the results are devastating. Why compound the pain with the belief that, not only is this upsetting, but it is also against some imaginary rule about the way things "should" be?

The belief that life "should" follow some doctrine of fairness or perfection is guaranteed to lead to aggravation and disappointment. And "shoulds" applied to yourself can cause increased anxiety. Such thoughts, including "I *should be* over these panic attacks by now" or "I *should be* strong enough to overcome anxiety without medication," are likely to cause more stress and pressure, rather than to solve the problem.

Always Do Your Best?

Simple phrases that parents use may set us up to feel more anxiety than necessary. Some parents say "Always do your best" not realizing that, after taking the best shower, making their bed in the most attractive way, having the healthiest breakfast, approaching everyone with the most positive attitude, and giving their all to any task with which they are presented, most children will face exhaustion before noon. We need to be sensitive to the pressure that we put on ourselves through our thought processes. Take some time to identify the thoughts that regularly dominate your perspective on life, and evaluate their impact on you. When you have more realistic expectations of yourself and those around you, you will not feel that so many events and situations are fraught with danger.

When you recognize that certain thought processes activate the amygdala's warning system, you can take steps to prevent yourself from unnecessarily activating the amygdala. If you keep your cortex focused on positive or neutral thoughts, you are reducing the likelihood that your amygdala will respond as if there is a present danger.

We may not be able to control the triggers we encounter in the external world, but we certainly have some control over the internal triggers that we allow to invade our thoughts. We can keep ourselves from constantly watching the Anxiety Channel and from having expectations that set us up for more stress.

Replace, Because You Can't Erase

When attempting to control thoughts, a common complaint people express is that they cannot get rid of the negative thoughts. This is because trying to erase or silence a thought is not an effective approach. If you are asked to stop thinking about pink elephants, for example, the image of pink elephants leaps into your mind. The harder you remind yourself to stop thinking about pink elephants, the more you think of them. Erasing a thought simply by thinking about doing so just doesn't work.

You can successfully interrupt a thought by specifically telling yourself "Stop!" This interrupts the thought, but the next step is crucial. If you *replace* the thought with another thought, you will be more likely to keep the first thought out of your mind. If you are driving, for example, and you keep thinking about potential accidents that could happen, tell yourself "Stop!" and then begin thinking about something else: the song on the radio, a project that you are doing at work, or the names of the flowers in the gardens on your route. By replacing the anxiety-provoking thought with something that is engaging your mind with other matters, you are making it more likely that you will not return to that thought. Once again, the idea of changing the channel is a helpful image to keep in mind.

"**Don't Erase - Replace!**" is also important with the Self-Defeating Thoughts. Telling yourself to stop thinking that you need to be perfectly competent is not as effective as replacing the thought with a Coping Thought. If you keep telling yourself "Nobody's perfect, so don't be hard on yourself," you are practicing a more adaptive way of thinking. You will be changing your thoughts from those that create anxiety to those that protect you from additional anxiety that you tend to create for yourself. It takes some practice, but the new thoughts eventually become habits.

How about a Distraction?

Negative thoughts can be like a snowball rolling downhill, getting larger and picking up speed until your amygdala notices you're stressed and sounds the alarm. Another very simple cognitive technique that can be used to put the brakes on anxiety is distraction. **Distraction** refers to the process of focusing your attention on anything other than the triggers that increase your anxiety. Literally, anything. If getting your blood drawn makes you nervous, attempt to distract yourself from the situation by listening to music, reading the posters on the wall, doing a crossword puzzle, or talking to the person next to you. Distraction occupies your thoughts with something that keeps you from focusing on the cues that elicit anxiety. You can distract yourself from external cues, like the sight of the syringe, as well as from internal cues, such as thoughts about possibly passing out, losing control, or being embarrassed. Before you know it, the situation is over.

One important point to note: Distraction should **not** be used during exposure exercises. Using distraction during exposure is counterproductive because it will prevent the extinction process from occurring. So, *during exposure exercises do not use distraction.* Save distraction for situations where it will have a positive effect.

For example, distraction is very useful in coping with anticipation. **Anticipation** refers to thoughts and feelings that we experience before an event - when we think ahead to something that might happen or is going to happen. For individuals with anxiety, anticipation is often a very unpleasant experience. How many of us have had a worrisome meeting scheduled at 1 p.m., and spent all morning anticipating and worrying about the meeting? Or perhaps you began worrying the night before, sacrificing hours of sleep? In either case, we have been watching the Anxiety Channel for too long! Instead of having a stressful experience for an hour or so during the meeting, we suffer through hours of anxiety imagining what could be said or what could go wrong. Many times we develop elaborate responses to potential situations that never even happen!

Anticipation is often more agonizing than the event itself. This is because we can imagine far worse outcomes than those that actually occur. We can also exhaust ourselves with worries before the event ever arrives. In addition, anticipation exposes the amygdala to anxiety-provoking thoughts and images even though, at the time, we are in a very safe situation. If you are anticipating an event and feeling anxious, try to distract yourself from thinking about the event. If your morning is filled with activities that distract you from an upcoming afternoon appointment, you won't spend your time thinking about negative outcomes and getting your amygdala in an uproar. Or, if you know that you must eat dinner with an unpleasant person, focus your thoughts on other people prior to the dinner, so that you have the unpleasant person on your mind for the shortest time possible.

Of course, there are times when you need to focus on an upcoming event, such as when you must write a speech or make travel arrangements. If you do these preparations well in advance, and allow yourself to use distraction as the important date or appointment approaches, you are less likely to be overwhelmed by anxiety. For instance, it is helpful to buy plane tickets long before a flight and then distract yourself from worrying about the trip as it approaches. This minimizes the overall anxiety that you experience. Distraction cannot be used at every moment, but it can reduce the amount of time that you focus your thoughts on images or ideas that activate your amygdala. Minimize your time on the Anxiety Channel. There are so many other great channels to watch!

Use of Medications in Cognitive Approaches

When you try to modify your thinking processes, you may find that your thoughts seem resistant to change. This is very common, but it does not mean that you should give up. Like habits, thoughts can be changed with some effort. If you continue to repeat certain thoughts in your head, eventually they will become second nature. But some individuals find that medications may give them assistance in changing their thinking habits. In fact, some medications may be useful to take during a period of months in which a person is trying to change his or her thoughts about anxiety-related situations.

You may recall that in Chapter 9, we described the SSRIs as medications that promote flexibility in thinking processes. Since SSRIs may lead to changes in the structure of neurons in the brain, they may increase the brain's ability to restructure parts of itself. This could make the brain more likely to learn. For this reason, SSRIs may be helpful when you are attempting to use some of the cognitive approaches described in this chapter. After you have established a new pattern of thinking, you can work with your doctor to gradually taper off the medication, but the new patterns of thinking will remain. This is not to say that medications are necessary for cognitive approaches to work, only that they may make your thinking more flexible and responsive to your efforts to change.

Increased flexibility in thinking is often a useful effect of medications like SSRIs. Increased flexibility does not directly reduce anxiety, but it gives a person more control over thought processes that might impact anxiety. However, if a person is unaware of what cognitive methods to use in changing anxiety-producing thoughts, the medication by itself is not as likely to help. Increased flexibility is wasted when a person does not know what to change in his or her thinking.

Remember the analogy from Chapter 9? Putting fertilizer in your garden will promote the growth of both weeds and vegetables if you don't know the difference between the two. But if a person knows what thoughts to weed out, and what thoughts to cultivate, the "fertilizer" provided by SSRIs can be effective. Combining cognitive approaches with medications like SSRIs may result in quicker, more effective change in anxiety-producing thoughts than using either approach on its own. And you don't need to maintain the "fertilizer" by continuing to take the medication once the new thoughts are firmly planted in your brain. As we noted, you can gradually taper off the medications once you have modified your pattern of thoughts, and your new patterns of thinking will remain.

When Thoughts Add to Anxiety

Thoughts are not always the source of our anxiety, as we know. Sometimes the source of anxiety is a situation or sensation, such as having to enter a small elevator, or feeling lightheaded. Even in these situations, however, your thoughts can still have a significant impact on your ability to deal with your anxiety in a way that helps, or makes it worse. Certain thoughts, such as "This space is so tiny, I can't breathe" or "I'm sure I'll pass out and no one will help me" are clearly self-defeating. You will benefit from monitoring your thoughts and making every effort to avoid thoughts that make the situation seem worse than it is.

Recognize ways in which you increase the perceived threat of situations by the way that you think about them, and make a conscious effort to avoid such thoughts completely. Arguing with them by saying "The last time I rode in an elevator, everything was fine" or "I've felt this way before, but I've never passed out" is one approach, but this still keeps your brain on the Anxiety Channel. Another approach is to change the channel completely by distracting yourself and not thinking about the situation at all. Focus your mind on something that totally diverts your attention. Try to concentrate on something external to yourself that you can get engrossed in, even temporarily. You can use simple exercises like counting backwards by sevens or trying to find everything in the room that is blue. You can listen to music on your MP3 player or play a handheld electronic game. Like a snowball rolling downhill – getting larger and picking up speed – negative thoughts can build until your amygdala notices them and sounds the alarm. Distraction helps to interrupt this process and keeps you calm.

Some of us have our anxiety-creating moments after an event occurs. When something goes wrong, we feel that we have just experienced a catastrophe. **Catastrophizing** occurs when someone thinks that a small setback is a major difficulty. If you have lost your temper as a result of being stopped by a red light, or have completely panicked when you couldn't find your keys for a couple of minutes, you have been catastrophizing. We let our thoughts run away with us and say things like "Now I'll never get there on time!" or "I'm going to be locked out forever!" when the truth is much less disastrous. Replacing the catastrophizing thought "I'll never get there!" with a more realistic thought like "This stop light will add approximately one minute to my trip," can greatly reduce anxiety.

Certain kinds of thoughts have been identified to be characteristic of anxious individuals. For example, individuals with agoraphobia often interpret their physical symptoms (such as breathing difficulties and stomach distress) as dangerous. Individuals with social phobia are very sensitive to the possibility of rejection from others. Those with Generalized Anxiety Disorder are prone to excessive worry. Knowing your own tendencies can help you to identify problematic thoughts to target in your own life. If you recognize yourself beginning to think about your breathing, try to change the focus of your thinking completely by becoming involved in a game or television show. If you find yourself considering that someone is disappointed in you, don't dwell on these thoughts, but start a conversation on another topic with a friend. If you find yourself worrying, go out and rake your yard and focus on deciding what bulbs you want to plant for the spring. Make use of your higher level thinking processes in order to direct your attention and thoughts away from the anxiety-building thoughts that trigger your own anxious reactions.

Play!

One of the most effective approaches we have found to work for cognitive distraction is play. So many individuals suffering from anxiety disorders are gripped with an excruciating seriousness. They take life so seriously that they have difficulty loosening up and having fun. Cultivating a sense of playfulness is essential.

To be able to joke and play adds so much to life. And it isn't necessary to wait until you have overcome anxiety to become playful. In fact, becoming playful is one of the best ways to overcome anxiety. Humor is essential in coping with life's challenges. So don't wait until it feels safe enough to play, or until you feel relaxed or happy enough to joke. Be playful in order to find relaxation, humor, and happiness.

Chapter 11
Putting It All Together:
A Whole Brain Approach to Anxiety

Keeping the Big Picture in Mind

We have written this book with the intention of giving you the knowledge and resources that you need to reach the goals you set for yourself in life. When your anxiety blocks you from your goals, we want you to have the strategies you need to overcome anxiety. We want you to be able to change your brain so that you aren't limited by fears and anxieties. This will be a challenge, but you will find yourself more successful if you use your **whole brain** in overcoming anxiety.

Remember that what you are hoping to accomplish is to make lasting changes in your brain necessary to modify your anxiety responses. Because you know the amygdala is the underlying source of all fear and anxiety responses, you recognize that knowing the language of the amygdala is the key to being successful in this endeavor. Through specific experiences, you are trying to provide your amygdala with the opportunities that it needs to learn a new way of responding.

At the same time, you are making use of your cerebral cortex. This book is written to your cerebral cortex, which allows you to read, learn, and remember how anxiety functions in your brain. You also use your cerebral cortex to exercise control over your cognitive or thinking processes, so that you don't allow them to worsen your anxiety and fear as you work on changing your brain.

The combined use of your cerebral cortex and the language of the amygdala is a very potent treatment approach. Many therapists target only the cerebral cortex, focusing on changing thinking in order to reduce anxiety. This method does not consider the whole brain. Although making changes in your thinking processes can be helpful in modifying some aspects of anxiety, to be effective you also need to consider the role of the amygdala. Changes in thinking cannot be completely effective because anxiety can be produced by the amygdala without the influence of any thinking at all. A clear understanding of the *role of the amygdala* and the *influence of the cerebral cortex* is essential in the process of using your whole brain to overcome the limits of anxiety.

Don't Go It Alone

We strongly recommend that you seek professional help as you work on the strategies presented in this book. The kind of assistance that will prove most helpful is cognitive behavioral therapy, because cognitive behavioral therapists are trained in identifying self-defeating thoughts as well as in exposure therapy. Cognitive behavioral therapists may come from a variety of disciplines, like social work or psychology, for example. The important question for you to ask when choosing a therapist is whether your therapist is knowledgeable about cognitive behavioral methods of treatment. A therapist with this background can assist you in a variety of ways as you carry out the strategies recommended in this book.

Specifically, a cognitive behavioral therapist will be familiar with how to approach exposure. A therapist who can assist you in identifying triggers and deciding which ones are important to target in exposure exercises is very valuable in this process. Having some assistance in determining which triggers most impair your ability to reach your goals in life allows you to target your efforts most effectively.

Learning relaxation skills may also be easier with a professional's assistance. Therapists can be helpful in providing encouragement, reminding you of what you are trying to accomplish, and highlighting your successes, too. Therapists who have experience with exposure can offer suggestions for responding to difficulties that arise in exposure exercises. Their expertise will assist you in making exposure exercises more effective. Finally, cognitive behavioral therapists are very adept at recognizing self-defeating thoughts and suggesting coping thoughts to replace them, so they can help you to use your cortex to combat anxiety.

Consider This:

Do you have a therapist with whom you can discuss your difficulties with anxiety? Does the therapist have training in cognitive behavioral therapy, including use of exposure therapy and identification of self-defeating thoughts? Can you discuss the "language of the amygdala" with your therapist?

While it is possible that you can accomplish many of the goals you set without a therapist, don't underestimate the challenge that you are facing. Having a skilled therapist is a very valuable resource. When facing the complex difficulties that anxiety brings, it is helpful to have a non-anxious brain available to assist in the process. And if the other brain helping you also understands the language of the amygdala, so much the better!

Prepare Your Brain For Learning

As you begin working on changing your brain by teaching your cortex new habits of thinking and providing your amygdala with new experiences, make sure your brain is ready for learning. You can best prepare your brain by making sure that it is healthy and rested. Make sure that you are eating a good, balanced diet, which will help you to remain alert and not sluggish.

You should also make sure that you get quality sleep. Sleep is important for two reasons. First, when you don't get enough sleep, your amygdala is much more reactive than when you are well rested. In fact, research has shown that when a person is sleep deprived, even for one evening, the amygdala reacts much more strongly to negative stimulation, and the cortex seems to have difficulty maintaining any influence in the situation.[1] Second, sleep is also essential for changing your brain. It is during sleep that our memories are formed and carefully stored by our brains.[2] Sleep-deprived brains don't form memories as well as rested brains do. As you try to provide your brain with new experiences, in hopes of rewiring the brain's circuitry, you need to sleep well so that those experiences are transformed into memories that will last.

Consider This:

Have you ever noticed how a lack of sleep can influence your moods? Do you find that you are more edgy or anxious when you have not had enough sleep? How many hours of sleep per night do you need to feel rested?

Another way of preparing the brain for change is to consider what substances are affecting the brain. The use of recreational substances, including **alcohol**, can impair the brain's ability to learn, and may make it difficult to change your anxiety responses. Even though certain substances like alcohol can help us to get through an anxious experience, they do not change the underlying brain processes that cause the anxiety. They are only a band-aid approach to the problem, covering it up, but doing nothing to promote new learning.

Caffeine can also have a strong effect on the brain, increasing activation of certain neurons, and promoting adrenaline release. Use of caffeine can contribute to symptoms of anxiety, and is best avoided when you want to minimize anxious responding.

In a similar way, you should consider what medications you are taking as you attempt to change your brain's anxiety responses. As you recall from Chapter 9, some medications will impair the brain's ability to create new circuitry, and some medications may actually assist the creation of new circuitry. It is important that you and your doctor or therapist know the specific effects of the medication that you are taking.

Medications in the Whole Brain Approach

When you recognize that your goal is to make lasting changes in your brain, you should view the use of medications in a new light. Certain medications, like benzodiazepines, have the ability to reduce our anxiety in minutes, but they actually impair the brain's ability to learn and change itself. So, even though we feel better in the short term, we are not making any changes in the brain's circuitry. These medications "cool" the anxiety-producing circuitry in the brain, which provides a great sense of immediate relief, but they are also "freezing" the brain in its current state. Nothing has changed. The same associations are maintained in the amygdala.

If you want to include medications in the process of modifying your anxiety responses, the first step is to communicate with your psychiatrist about what you are attempting to accomplish. If a family practitioner is prescribing your medications, we strongly suggest that you seek the help of a psychiatrist during this process. Psychiatrists have more experience with the specific medications used to treat anxiety because they are specialists in treating psychological disorders. They also know more about the brain, and how medications affect it, than do most family practice physicians. In addition, psychiatrists are more likely to be familiar with cognitive behavioral approaches, including exposure and the use of cognitive therapy for self-defeating thoughts.

This is not to imply that psychiatrists are trained in cognitive behavioral methods. Psychiatrists are trained in the administration of medications, and very few have extensive training in cognitive behavioral therapy or other psychotherapy methods. Many individuals seeking treatment for anxiety expect their psychiatrists to provide therapy, and are surprised that psychiatrists focus primarily on the use of medication. The reason is that psychiatrists are not therapists. They are *physicians* trained to treat psychological disorders (largely through the use of medications). You should expect your psychiatrist to be your best resource in terms of understanding how medications affect you and your brain, but you should not expect your psychiatrist to be trained in therapeutic techniques.

As you speak with your psychiatrist about the medications you are taking or are considering taking, make a distinction between those medications that provide relief from anxiety on a short term basis, and those which can assist you in modifying your brain's anxiety responses in a more lasting way. Refer to Chapter 9. Inform your psychiatrist about any side effects you are experiencing from the medications, and explain the approaches you are using in combating anxiety. Communication between your psychiatrist and your therapist can also help facilitate the process of changing your anxious brain. All three of you (the psychiatrist, the therapist, and you) can make important contributions in the process of evaluating how a medication is working, and how it affects the treatment process.

Consider This:

Are you comfortable talking with your physician or psychiatrist about your medications, including how they work (in both the short term and long term) and what side effects they produce? Do you have a therapist who can assist you in evaluating whether the medications are having the effects that you are seeking?

Where Do I Begin?

The many strategies described in this book may leave you wondering how to begin the process of using the whole brain approach. The best way to start is with **Relaxation**, as explained in Chapter 7. Learn the skill of relaxing yourself by turning off your sympathetic nervous system and activating your parasympathetic nervous system. Don't forget to consider exercise in achieving relaxation, as well. Use relaxation repeatedly during each day so that your overall anxiety level becomes generally lower. Integrate relaxation methods into your life so that it becomes second nature to relax yourself several times each day.

Next, become aware of how your thoughts contribute to your anxiety. Look for **Self-Defeating Thoughts** and identify how they turn up in a variety of situations. Recognize how certain thoughts increase the activation of your amygdala by suggesting that there is more danger than is actually present. Tune out the **Anxiety Channel!** Work to replace your self-defeating thoughts with **Coping Thoughts** that reduce your anxiety and calm your fears, as explained in Chapter 10. Practice monitoring and modifying your thoughts until you can consistently think in more productive ways in most situations. Consider whether certain medications may be helpful in this process, because, as we noted in Chapter 9, some medications (especially the SSRIs) have been shown to increase cognitive flexibility.

As you consider what aspects of your life you want to change, it is essential that you identify what **Life Goals** are important to you and what fears are keeping you from pursuing these goals. Target the fears that are blocking you. Review Chapter 8 to help you identify **Triggers** for fear and decide what triggers you want to focus on first. Use the language of the amygdala to change your brain's response to these triggers, so that these triggers will no longer create responses that block you from your goals.

Finally, begin using **Exposure** techniques like those detailed in Chapters 5 and 6 to target your specific triggers. If you can associate these triggers with safety rather than anxiety, you can build bypasses and break the hold anxiety has over your life. Make sure that you use all that you know about relaxation, self-defeating thoughts, and coping thoughts to assist you as you work through the exposure experiences with your therapist. Remember to expose yourself to each situation in your **hierarchy** until you feel your fear markedly decrease. Repeat exposure exercises often until you are relatively comfortable with the situation.

When you feel stressed by the exposure exercises you are undertaking, remind yourself that you must activate parts of your amygdala to generate new connections in your brain. The phrase "**Activate to Generate**" is a reminder that you cannot make new connections in your brain unless you experience some anxiety. Work toward reducing anxiety surrounding any trigger that is blocking your goals until you feel more in control. Be aware of the importance of varying the **context** during exposure and try exposure in different settings. Finally, be careful of the negative effects of **safety-seeking behavior** as explained in Chapter 6.

In summary, the process of changing your brain to resist anxiety is a gradual one, but your brain will slowly adapt itself to the experiences that you expose it to, and will learn to respond in new ways. Your brain is sensitive and responsive to its environment. It will modify itself if it is given the proper learning experiences.

Relaxation and exercise will help increase parasympathetic activation, reducing your body's stress response. Through this whole brain approach, elimination of self-defeating thoughts will eventually change your cortex's responding, and exposure experiences will gradually change your amygdala's responding. No doubt there will be set backs along the way, but you will see an improvement in your ability to take charge of your life if you make use of these strategies.

You Can Do It!

Although this process may seem overwhelming, if you break it down into steps, it is much more manageable. Try to focus on one aspect of the process at a time. You will see improvements at each step that will encourage you. When you see that you are able to relax yourself, you will feel more confident about managing your anxiety. And when you experience how exposure is steadily reducing your fear, you will begin to develop the ability to push through your fears with confidence.

Keep in mind that your ultimate goal is to retrain your brain, so try to remember what is happening in your brain at each step. Every strategy that you use sends an important message to your brain, and your brain will respond. Many strategies require repetition, but that is typical of many personal goals in life, from arithmetic to athletics. Just keep in mind that you are using your whole brain to resist the controlling effects of anxiety. You are taking charge of your life, step by step.

Summary of Strategies

- Use **Breathing** and **Relaxation** techniques to reduce sympathetic activation.
- Monitor thinking for **Self-Defeating Thoughts**.
- Replace Self-Defeating Thoughts with **Coping Thoughts**.
- Determine **Life Goals** and when anxiety interferes with these goals.

- Identify **Triggers** for fears and anxiety that interfere with your goals.
- Design **Exposure Exercises** that can modify your amygdala's response to these triggers.
- **Activate to Generate** new circuitry to build a bypass in your amygdala.
- **Practice** Exposure Exercises until you recognize a considerable decrease in your anxiety and fear.
- Change the **Context** of your exposure exercises to get the most benefit.
- Watch out for **Safety-Seeking behaviors,** and use **medication** wisely.
- **Relax** and enjoy life!

Chapter 12
Change Your Mind to Change Your Brain

Philosophical and Spiritual Approaches to Anxiety

In our whole brain approach, it would be a mistake if we did not address the fact that a person's philosophical and spiritual approach to life also impacts his or her anxiety. We have found that certain perspectives are likely to worsen a person's anxiety, while other perspectives help a person to cope. In this chapter, we will provide you with some philosophical and spiritual perspectives on anxiety that may improve your ability to take control of your life.

We have found one of the most useful approaches to anxiety in Reinhold Niebuhr's Serenity Prayer. Most people are familiar with the prayer:

> *God grant me the **serenity** to accept the things I cannot change*
> *The **courage** to change the things I can*
> *And the **wisdom** to know the difference.*

While coping with the complex and multifaceted experience of anxiety, we find it very helpful to consider that certain aspects of anxiety can be changed quite readily, while other aspects are difficult, if not impossible, to change. For example, a person is typically able to interrupt some of the behaviors associated with anxiety, such as hyperventilating, quite readily. Changing self-defeating thoughts is more challenging, but definitely achievable. On the other hand, keeping your amygdala from triggering the release of adrenaline in many anxiety-provoking situations is sometimes impossible.

We are hopeful that this book has helped you to gain the wisdom to know what you can change and what you simply need to accept. As you read this book, you learned what aspects of anxiety are beyond a person's control. For example, you cannot tell yourself to stop feeling anxiety, and expect it to simply happen, since your brain is based on centuries of evolution that wired your brain and your body to respond in this manner. Knowing the ability of the amygdala to override many of your best intentions, you realize that you have limits.

Although we can help you to reduce the number of times you experience anxiety, we cannot give you any way to guarantee that you will not have anxious moments and the accompanying sensations that you know so well. Hopefully, because of what you have learned about how the brain creates anxiety, you can accept the experience as something that is extremely uncomfortable at times, but not dangerous to you. In fact, the experience of anxiety means your body is trying to protect you, not to harm you.

You also learned that certain aspects of anxiety are capable of being modified. You can change some things pretty easily by focusing on relaxing your muscles or distracting yourself, for example. Other changes take much more time and effort, such as undertaking a series of exposure exercises in order to extinguish your fear of certain triggers. Some of these changes require a great deal of courage, as the serenity prayer suggests.

The serenity prayer reminds us that we cannot change the fact that our brains are designed to produce anxiety. We should not consider ourselves weak or foolish because we have certain fears or a high level of anxiety. We need to accept the fact that we are each born with a specific brain which may be more or less vulnerable to anxiety. We also know that the brain we have has often been influenced by experiences beyond our control.

We don't have to accept this brain as incapable of change, however. We do have ways to influence what our brains learn. Even the most anxious brain can learn to be less anxious, if you know the language of the amygdala, and use your cortex to keep anxiety under control.

The more that we know about how our brains learn fear and anxiety, the more we can sort out what we can and cannot control - and the more we are able to achieve the goals we set for ourselves. If we evaluate, sometimes on a daily basis, what aspects of anxiety we can and cannot control, we will be better able to decide how to approach a given situation. It is beneficial to use the serenity prayer frequently, because a variety of dynamic factors impact how difficult it is to make a change. Further, the influence of these factors varies depending on the specific situation.

Our hope is that the information in this book has helped you to clarify what you can change, as well as what is too difficult or impossible to change, so that you may find a healthy balance between challenging and accepting your anxiety.

Take a moment to go back and re-read the serenity prayer. For us, the prayer means to accept, in as relaxed and serene a manner as possible, that anxiety is part of your daily life. Do not make it worse by worrying about it or punishing yourself over it. Carefully consider what you want to change in your life, and have the courage that it takes to make the changes that can be made. Change is not easy, but we have tried to provide you with the knowledge you will need to attempt it. Use this knowledge wisely. If you have courage, you can change a great deal.

Acceptance

A variety of contemplative practices can be helpful, including prayer, meditation, chanting, yoga, and simple silent time. An important skill to possess, which is part of many contemplative practices, is the skill of **acceptance**. Acceptance can be very useful in coping with anxiety. When we have stressful experiences, we can make them worse by trying to fight or deny the feelings that we are having. Sometimes the best thing to do is to simply accept that we are feeling lousy and get through it.

Remind yourself that you don't have to pretend that you are fine; you can admit that you are suffering, anxious, or afraid. It can be such a relief to admit this. It takes a great deal of energy to cover up your feelings. When you accept your experiences and don't have to pretend that you are all right, you save yourself a great deal of effort. Sometimes we are overly concerned about how others will react, but the truth is that others often give us more understanding and support when we admit that we are having difficulties.

Acceptance involves simply being aware of the feelings and experiences that you are having, and not over-analyzing them or worrying about what they mean. For example, you can feel your heart beating or feel light-headed without trying to analyze what these sensations imply or worrying whether they are dangerous. They are simply sensations resulting from the stress response when activated by your overly enthusiastic amygdala. You can experience them as they occur, being aware, but not overly concerned.

Consider This:

What are you typically thinking about when you are experiencing anxiety symptoms? Do you find yourself evaluating or analyzing the symptoms and worrying about what they mean? How do these thoughts affect your anxiety level?

Mindfulness

A technique called **mindfulness**, which is often used by those who meditate, is useful when working toward acceptance. The goal of mindfulness is to be aware of what is happening in your mind and body. Mindfulness is not thinking, or interpreting, or judging. It is simply calm observation of your experience. Your experience is something that you are *having*, it is not you. When you apply this to anxiety, it means that you may be feeling anxious, but anxiety does not control all of you. *You can watch yourself have the experience rather than get caught up in it.* For example, you may say to yourself "My anxiety is fairly strong right now, and I can feel my heart pounding," yet remain aware of and accepting of the experience. When you are mindful, you don't try to figure out why or try to change the experience. You simply acknowledge the situation and let it be.

Investigators are trying to determine what happens in the brain when attention is focused on our experience in this way. A variety of techniques from EEGs to MRIs have been used to study changes that occur in the brain as a person engages in mindful meditation, and specific changes in brain functioning have been observed. Meditation often seems to be accompanied by increased activity in the left prefrontal cortex, often associated with positive emotions, and a decrease in the activity of areas in the brain associated with our awareness of the location of our body (the parietal cortex).[1] However, the results are too preliminary to allow us to understand exactly what happens in the brain when we focus on being mindful. We know that the brain changes its activity in response to mindfulness, but we don't yet know exactly how to characterize this change.

The experiential goal of mindfulness is to transform the focus of your awareness. A mindful perspective allows you to get in touch with a more calm, observing part of yourself that is above your anxiety. You don't allow yourself to focus on any specific goal or agenda. You just observe. Mindfulness teaches us that all of our experiences are transient and temporary. You can say to yourself "My anxiety will rise, but eventually it will go back down" as you observe the process.

This kind of acceptance of one's feelings has been shown to be helpful for those coping with anxiety. For example, a group of anxiety-sensitive individuals were given carbon dioxide enriched air, which often increases feelings of fear in those who are anxiety-sensitive. Those who were encouraged to mindfully observe their thoughts and feelings reported less fear and fewer catastrophic thoughts than those who were asked to control their symptoms through diaphragmatic breathing.[2] This suggests that if you work toward acceptance of some symptoms, rather than focusing on controlling them all, you may find yourself experiencing less anxiety in the long run.

Further, it is important to remind yourself that you will get through the situation. You have survived similar experiences in the past, and you know that you can do it. This is also part of acceptance.

Mindfulness and acceptance involve, perceiving and acknowledging the anxiety, fear or distress you are feeling, then, getting through it. We often dedicate a great deal of energy to avoiding our anxiety and fear, when it may be more effective simply to *push through* the experience. Try to observe your anxiety and let it flow through you until you come out "on the other side." Remember that one thing you can always count on is that your feelings will change. Feelings, by their nature, are temporary states. They won't last forever; neither will your anxiety.

Consider This:

Do you ever find yourself watching your anxiety and waiting for it to go away before you do something? Does it distract you from what you are trying to accomplish? Are you a hostage to your anxiety? What would happen if you could be aware of your anxiety, but not under its control?

Act Despite Anxiety

Acceptance does not mean that you let anxiety paralyze you. Mindfulness and acceptance are useful philosophical approaches that help us experience and live in the moment. This does not mean that you should stop pursuing goals that you have. In fact, you should pursue your goals *despite* the experience of anxiety, and even during the experience of anxiety. The desire to pursue your goals can be used as motivation to push through your anxiety and fear. Do not wait to live your life until your fears are gone. Instead, live your life despite your fear. Live your life with anxiety if necessary.

Courage is not the absence of fear. Courage is acting despite fear. The courageous person is not a person who approaches a situation without feeling anxious. What courage does that take? On the contrary, courage occurs when a person experiences fear or anxiety and acts despite the fear. We realize that this is very easily said, and very difficult to do. But the experience of acting in the face of fear is what true courage is about.

One Day at a Time

Another important philosophy that we encourage you to consider is the idea of taking life "one day at a time." In everyday practice, this means living in the present, and not allowing yourself to worry about what may or may not happen in the future. You can waste a great deal of time anticipating and worrying about events that may never even come to pass. A relevant quote from English banker and statesman Sir John Lubbock is worth considering: "A day of worry is more exhausting than a day of work." Keep your focus on today and you will save your mental energy for the tasks at hand.

"One day at a time" also suggests that you need to let go of yesterday's difficulties, and not drag them with you as you continue living your life. You can sometimes ruin a perfectly safe and comfortable day by bringing yesterday's difficulties into it. Try to make it your goal to enjoy every day, to play, and to live in the moments that you have. Don't spoil a perfectly good moment by dwelling on unpleasant memories rather than focusing on the moment at hand.

You don't need to think about any more challenges or difficulties than the ones that are right in front of you. Don't create additional suffering and anxiety for yourself by thinking about more than one day at a time. Keep in mind that your amygdala often has difficulty distinguishing between real dangers and the dangers you imagine. Why would you want to relive stressful events of the past, or frighten yourself about the future, by constantly tuning in to the Anxiety Channel? There are so many more interesting and pleasurable channels to focus your attention on. You can miss some of the best experiences in your life by keeping yourself focused on the Anxiety Channel.

<u>*Consider This:*</u>

> *Do you know anyone who is particularly skilled at living in the moment? Consider how others allow themselves to let go and experience each day, despite past hardships or impending difficulties. Try to follow their example.*

A corollary to the idea of "one day at a time" that is useful in moments of stress is to recognize the advantage of focusing on "one minute at a time." In some situations we find ourselves experiencing a high level of anxiety. When someone asks, "What are you going to do this afternoon?" or "When are you going to do the shopping?" we suddenly feel extremely overwhelmed. Sometimes getting through a specific moment is all that we can handle.

It is perfectly reasonable to focus on coping with one situation at a time. Luckily, life is presented to us one minute at a time. (Actually, maybe one second at a time?) All we need to do is to get through each minute. When struggling with anxiety, getting through some of the tough minutes is an achievement in and of itself! So, being able to say, "I have all I can deal with right now, and I'll need to think about that later" can make a situation more manageable. Take life one minute at a time whenever necessary and you will find life easier to manage.

Focus on the Positive

Your life is made up of many moments, and if you can learn to focus your brain on the positive ones, and to savor them, you will feel much happier. Difficulties may return in the future, but so will pleasure. Learn to relish the moments filled with joy when they come, and hold on to those experiences. Cultivate playfulness. Cherish the ones you love. We know from experience that love is stronger than fear.

Setbacks will come in life, but they are simply a sign that you are testing the limits. Of course, ships are safe in the harbor, but they aren't built to remain in the harbor. They are built to sail. If you never have a setback, you are probably not trying. But it is not necessary to *dwell* on your setbacks. Accept them and move on.

You can find beauty and pleasure in life if you look for it. Just make it your goal to savor every moment. Consciously experience every happy event using mindfulness, and feel the delight that you can get out of life's special times. Focus on playfulness and appreciate life's little pleasures: people you love, food you enjoy, beauty that you see.

Make it your goal to find joy and to have fun - whether or not anxiety is a part of your life. Don't let fears and anxiety darken your view of the world. What you focus your thinking on has a very powerful influence on your brain. Focus your brain on the positive, beautiful, and pleasurable aspects of your life and your brain will be happier as a result.

This Isn't Fair!

As we stated in Chapter 10, don't get caught up in believing that life should be fair. The truth is that life is not fair; when we expect it to be fair we will always be disappointed. Unfortunately, we each have to play the game of life with the hand we have been dealt. All we can do is to make the best of what we were dealt. No one knows the best way for you to play that hand. It's your call.

Other people may not be able to completely understand what you are going through, but it will help if at least *you* understand. If you recognize what you are dealing with when you are coping with anxiety, it helps. Some people don't think twice about driving to work each morning, while other people face more feelings of terror before lunch than most people do all year. Your family may not recognize that for you, getting to home plate means running six or seven bases, not just four - but if you realize that, and give yourself credit, it can help a great deal. What you achieve will mean that much more given that you have had to contend with anxiety that others don't even think about.

Don't Mind Your Anxiety

Whether we were born with brains that create anxiety or acquired our anxiety problems due to experiences we've had, we can use mindfulness to cope with anxiety. We can try to focus our thoughts on the positive, and to keep ourselves from being controlled by anxiety. All of the knowledge you have gained by reading this book can help you to find effective ways to manage your anxious brain. We hope that you use this book to find relief, encouragement, and joy in your life. You deserve it!

Appendix A

Diagrams (Answers from page 46)

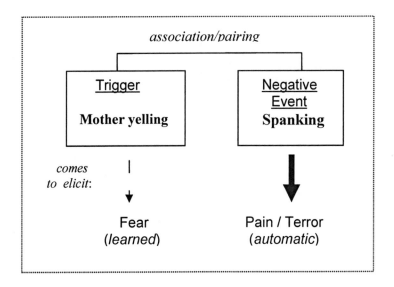

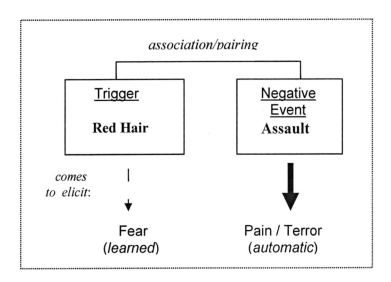

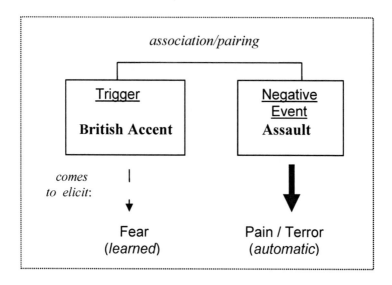

Appendix B

Relaxation Instructions

Begin each relaxation session by focusing your attention on your breathing for a few moments. Slow your breathing down and deepen it. Remember to use diaphragmatic breathing (from Chapter 5). Do not hold your breath. Just lengthen your inhalation and exhalation by breathing slowly. If you can slow your breathing to five or six breaths per minute, it will promote relaxation.

Sometimes it helps if you think of a word like "relax" or "peace" as you are breathing deeply and slowly. Others find it useful to use imagery. Perhaps imagine that with each breath, you are breathing out the stress you may feel, and breathing in clean air. Imagine that the stress is a color (perhaps black or red) and that you are breathing it out, filling yourself with clear, stress-free colorless air.

Breathing is not just the first step you should focus on, but should be a constant focus throughout the relaxation process. Keep your breathing slow and deep as you turn to the second step. The second step is to focus on relaxing your muscles. Sitting in a firm chair is recommended.

Start with your hands. If you are going to use progressive relaxation, begin by tensing your muscles. This means making your hands into fists briefly. You should only tense briefly, and then try to completely relax your hand, including each of your fingers. If you are only focusing on relaxation without tensing your muscles, skip the tensing part and start at the next step: let your hands drop into your lap. Feel gravity pulling them down into your lap. Focus on releasing any tension in the muscles in your hands. You may need to wiggle your fingers to relax them. Concentrate on deepening the feeling of relaxation in your hands. Relaxation is a heavy feeling, pulling your hand down into your lap.

Next focus your attention on your forearms. If you are using progressive relaxation, you start by making a fist again. Also tighten up your forearm muscles to briefly create muscle tension in your forearm. Then, immediately drop your hands into your lap to allow the muscles in your hands and forearms to relax. Once again, if you are not including the tensing, begin by relaxing your forearm muscles. Focus on releasing any tension you feel in your forearms, and feel the heaviness of relaxation.

Then move to your upper arm or bicep. For progressive relaxation, start tensing your bicep by pulling your hand and forearm close to your upper arm. The next step (or the first step if you are simply relaxing your muscles) is to completely loosen and relax the bicep. It helps to promote relaxation of the bicep if you allow your arms to hang loosely at your sides. Allow the weight of your relaxed hand and arm to lengthen your bicep into a relaxed state. Shaking your arms to release tension is sometimes helpful.

Move to each muscle group below in turn, following a similar process. Include the tensing step if you wish, or exclude that and move directly to relaxing. With practice, you are likely to be able to eliminate the tensing part for all but the most stubbornly resistant muscles. But as you start to train yourself, tensing often helps to facilitate relaxation in muscles.

On the page below, you will find some suggestions for how to tense and relax each set of muscles. Don't forget to S-L-O-W and DEEPEN your breathing as you do these exercises.

Hands:
Tensing: Make a tight fist.
Relaxing: Allow hand to drop loosely into lap, and relax fingers.

Forearms:
Tensing: Make fist and tighten forearm muscles.
Relaxing: Drop your hands into your lap and relax arms.

Biceps:
Tensing: Pull hand and arm close to upper arm.
Relaxing: Allow arms to hang loosely at your sides.

Feet:
Tensing: Curl your toes.
Relaxing: Wiggle or stretch your toes.

Calves:
Tensing: Leave your heel on the ground and point your toes upward
Relaxing: Stretch your feet out into a comfortable position and relax your calves.

Thighs:
Tensing: Push your feet into the ground in order to tense your thighs.
Relaxing: Stretch your feet out again, and relax your calves and thighs.

Buttocks:
Tensing: Tighten your buttocks.
Relaxing: Sink comfortably into a relaxed position.

Forehead:
Tensing: Frown.
Relaxing: Lift eyebrows, then allow eyebrows to relax into a comfortable position.

Jaw, Tongue, Lips:
Tensing: Bite teeth together firmly, push tongue against teeth, push lips together
Relaxing: Open your mouth wide for a moment to stretch, then leave mouth open slightly, and relax tongue. Allow lips and tongue to be loose.

Neck:
Tensing: Tip head back.
Relaxing: Stretch neck by tipping head slowly from one side to the other, and tipping chin toward chest.

Shoulders:
Tensing: Bring shoulders up toward ears.
Relaxing: Allow weight of arms, hands to pull shoulders down.

<u>Stomach</u>:
Tensing: Tighten muscles as though you expected someone to punch you in the stomach
Relaxing: Allow your stomach muscles to be loose and take up as much space as they wish.

Appendix C

Imagery

When you use imagery to relax, you take yourself to another location in your imagination. Put simply, you are imagining yourself in another place. Start by slowing your breathing and relaxing your body as you mentally travel to another scene. Choose a location that you enjoy, close your eyes, and allow yourself to experience the sights and sounds of this special place. Focus on using all your senses (sight, sound, smell, touch, and even taste) as you imagine yourself in this particularly relaxing location.

Here is an example of some guided imagery to illustrate the technique:

Imagine yourself walking on a sandy path to a beach. As you walk on the path, you are surrounded by trees that keep you in dark shade. You feel the sand begin to get into your shoes as you walk along. You can hear the leaves in the trees softly moving in the wind, but up ahead, you hear another sound: the sound of gentle waves washing up on shore.

As you continue, you leave the shade of the trees to walk out onto a sunny, sandy beach. The sun warms your head and shoulders as you stand still for a moment to take in your surroundings. The sky is a clear blue, and wispy white clouds seem to hang motionless in the sky. You take off your shoes and feel the warm sand as your feet sink in. Holding your shoes, you move toward the water. The sound of the waves rhythmically washing up on the shore has a hypnotic quality. You breathe deeply, in unison with the waves.

The water is a dark blue, and you can see, far off, a darker blue line on the horizon where the water meets the light blue sky. In the distance, you see two sailboats, one with a white sail and one with a red sail; they appear to be racing one another. The damp smell of driftwood reaches your nose, and you see some nearby driftwood. You place your shoes on a smooth, weathered log and walk toward the waves.

Seagulls swoop overhead, and you hear their excited cries as they glide on the gentle breeze coming in with the waves. You feel the breeze on your skin and smell the freshness of the breeze. As you walk toward the waves, you see the sun reflected on the water. You walk into the damp sand, leaving footprints now as you walk along the shore. A wave breaks over your feet, surprisingly cold at first.

You stand still as the waves wash over your ankles. Listening to the repetitive sound of the waves and the cries of the gulls, you feel the wind blowing your hair away from your face. You take slow deep breaths of the cool, clean air...

Using imagery such as the scene described above, you can take a trip each day that is limited only by your imagination. As long as you focus on relaxing, pleasant images, it only takes a few minutes to decrease your sympathetic nervous system activation.

We recommend that you end each imagery session gradually, by counting backward slowly from ten to one. With each number, gradually become more aware of your surroundings, more aware of the actual sights and sounds around you. Finally, open your eyes. When you reach the count of one, return to the present feeling refreshed.

Notes

Chapter 1   About this Book

1. National Institute for Health and Clinical Excellence (2007); Forbes, Creamer, Phelps, Bryant, McFarlane, Devilly, Matthews, Raphael, Doran, Merlin, & Newton (2007); McLean, & Woody (2001).
2. Porto, Oliveira, Mari, Volchan, Figueira, & Ventura (2009).
3. Barlow (2002); Foa, Huppert, & Cahill (2006); Wolitzky-Taylor, Horowitz, Powers, & Telch (2008).

Chapter 2   Understanding What Causes Anxiety

1. See authors like Mark Bouton, Joseph LeDoux, Bruce S. Kapp, Susan Mineka, and Robert Sapolsky, for example.
2. Charney & Drevets (2002).
3. Sing, Stengard, & Kardia (2003).
4. Milham, Nugent, Drevets, Dickstein, Leibenluft, Ernst, Charney, & Pine (2005).
5. Neumeister, Bain, Nugent, Carson, Bonne, Luckenbaugh, Eckelman, Herscovitch, Charney, & Drevets (2004).
6. Mineka & Zinbarg (2006).
7. Kilpatrick, Koenen, Ruggiero, Acierno, Galea, Resnick, Roitzsch, Boyle, & Gelernter (2007).
8. Andreasen (2001), p. 35.

9. Bremner, Vythilingam, Vermetten, Adil, Khan, Nazeer, Afzal, McGlashan, Elzinga, Anderson Heninger, Southwick, & Charney (2003).
10. Mineka & Zinbarg (2006), p. 10.
11. Mineka & Zinbarg (2006).
12. Barlow (2002).

Chapter 3   How the Brain Creates Anxiety

1. LeDoux (1996).
2. Alvarez, Biggs, Chen, Pine, & Grillon (2008).
3. LeDoux (1996).
4. Gigerenzer (2004).
5. Bechara, Tranel, Damasio, & Adolphs (1995).
6. Claparede (1951).

Chapter 4   Fear and Anxiety in the Body

1. LeDoux (1996).
2. Sapolsky (1998).

Chapter 5   Exposure-Based Treatment:
Rewiring Your Brain

1. Wolitzky-Taylor, et al. (2008).
2. Foa, Huppert, & Cahill (2006).
3. Cain, Blouin, & Barad (2003).
4. Bouton (1994); Barad & Saxena, (2005).
5. Foa, et al. (2006).
6. Cahill, Franklin, & Feeney (2006).
7. Barad & Saxena (2005).

Chapter 6 Exposure-Based Treatment:
Factors to Consider

1. Bouton (1994).
2. Barad & Saxena (2005).
3. Barad & Saxena (2005).
4. Bouton (1993).
5. Bouton (1993).
6. Westra, Stewart, & Conrad (2002); Westra, Stewart, Teehan, Johl, Dozios, & Hill (2004).
7. Sloan & Telch (2002); Salkovskis, Clark, Hackmann, Wells, & Gelder (1999).
8. Salkovskis, et al. (1999) Thwaites & Freeston (2005).
9. Sloan & Telch (2002); Salkovskis, et al. (1999), Wells, Clark, Salkovkis, Ludgate, Hackmann, & Gelder (1995).
10. Foa, Huppert, & Cahill (2006).
11. Sloan & Telch (2002).

Chapter 7 Relaxation and Exercise

1. See for example, Bourne, Brownstein, & Garano (2004).
2. Jacobson (1938).
3. Bourne, et al. (2004).
4. Jacobson (1938).
5. Walsh & Shapiro (2006).
6. Allen, Blascovich, Tomaka, & Kelsey (1991).
7. Meredith, Friberg, Jennings, Dewar, Fazio, Lambert, & Esler (1991).

8. Petruzzello, Landers, Hatfield, Kubitz, & Salazar (1991).
9. Hale & Raglin (2002).
10. Crocker & Grozelle (1991).
11. Crocker & Grozelle (1991).
12. Johnsgard (2004).
13. Petruzzello, et al. (1991).
14. Thoren, Floras, Hoffman, & Seals (1990).
15. Hoffman, 1997, cited in Johnsgard (2004).
16. Bequet, Gomez-Merino, Berhelot, & Guezennec (2001).
17. Dishman (1997).
18. Bjornebekk, Mathe, & Brene (2005).
19. Petruzzello & Landers (1994).

Chapter 8   Know Yourself and Your Triggers

1. Cahill, Franklin, & Feeney (2006).

Chapter 9   Brain Medicine

1. Otto, Pollack, & Sabatino (1996).
2. *Physician's Desk Reference* (2004).
3. Coplan & Lydiard (1998).
4. Coplan & Lydiard (1998).
5. Tata, Rollings, Collins, Pickering, & Jacobson (1994); Westra, Stewart, Teehan, Johl, Dozios, & Hill (2004).
6. *Physician's Desk Reference* (2004).
7. Westra, Stewart, Teehan, Johl, Dozios, & Hill (2004).
8. Westra, Steward, & Conrad (2002); Ahmed, Westra, & Steward (2008)

9. Manji, Drevets, & Charney (2001); Charney & Drevets (2002).
10. Leonard (1997); Eisch, Cameron, Encinas, Meltzer, Ming, & Overstreet-Wediche (2008).
11. Manji, et al. (2001).
12. Wilkinson & Goodyer (2008).
13. Furmark, Tillsfors, Mateinsdottir, Fishcher, Pissiota, Langstrom, & Fredrikson (2002).
14. Carey, Warwick, Niehaus, van der Linden, van Heerden, Harvey, Seedat, & Stein (2004).
15. Nielson (1994).
16. Stein, Kerridge, Dimsdale, & Hoyt (2007); Vaiva, Ducrocq, Jezequel, Averland, Lestavel, Brunet, & Marmar (2003); Pitman, Sanders, Zusman, Healey, Cheema, Lasko, Cahill, & Orr (2002).
17. Liang (1999).
18. Tada, Kasamo, Ueda, Suzuki, Kojima, & Ishakawa (1999).
19. Davis, Myers, Ressler, & Rothbaum (2005).
20. Davis, Myers, Ressler, & Rothbaum (2005).
21. Guastella, Richardson, Lovibond, Rapee, Gaston, Mitchell, & Dadds (2008).
22. Davis, Myers, Ressler, & Rothbaum (2005).
23. Kushner, Kim, Donahue, Thuras, Adson, Kotlyar, McCabe, Peterson, & Foa (2007).

Chapter 10 Cognitive Approaches:
Using the Higher Levels of Your Brain

1. Dozois, Frewen, & Covin (2006).
2. Beck (2004), p. 200.
3. Beck (2004), p. 201.

Chapter 11   Putting It All Together:
A Whole Brain Approach to Anxiety

1. You, Gujar, Hu, Jolesz, & Walker (2007).
2. Drosopoulos, Schultze, Fischer, & Born (2007).

Chapter 12   Change Your Mind to Change Your Brain

1. Cardoso (2007).
2. Eifert & Heffner (2003).

References

Ahmed, M., Westra, H. A., & Stewart, S. H. (2008). A self-help handout for benzodiazepine discontinuation using cognitive behavior therapy. *Cognitive and Behavioral Practice, 15,* 317-324.

Allen, K. M., Blascovich, J., Tomaka, J., & Kelsey, R. M. (1991). Presence of human friends and pet dogs as moderators of autonomic responses to stress in women. *Journal of Personality and Social Psychology, 61,* 582-589.

Alvarez, R.P., Biggs, A., Chen, G., Pine, D.S., & Grillon, C. (2008). Contextual fear conditioning in humans: Cortical-hippocampal and amygdala contributions. *Journal of Neuroscience, 28,* 6211-6219.

Andreasen, N. C. (2001). *Brave New Brain: Conquering Mental Illness in the Era of the Genome.* New York, NY: Oxford University Press.

Barad, M. G., & Saxena, S. (2005). Neurobiology of extinction: A mechanism underlying behavior therapy for human anxiety disorders. *Primary Psychiatry, 12,* 45-51.

Barlow, D. H. (2002). *Anxiety and Its Disorders: The Nature and Treatment of Anxiety and Panic,* 2nd Edition. New York: Guilford.

Bechara, A., Tranel, D., Damasio, H., & Adolphs, R. (1995). Double dissociation of conditioning and declarative knowledge relative to the amygdala and hippocampus in humans. *Science, 269,* 1115-1118.

Beck , A. T. (2004). Cognitive therapy, behavior therapy, psychoanalysis, and pharmacotherapy: A cognitive continuum. In A. Freeman, M. J. Mahoney, P. Devito, & D. Martin (eds.), *Cognition and Psychotherapy, 2nd ed.*, pp. 197-220. New York: Springer Publishing Co.

Bequet, F., Gomez-Merino, D., Berhelot, M., & Guezennec, C. Y. (2001). Exercise-induced changes in brain glucose and serotonin revealed by microdialysis in rat hippocampus: Effect of glucose supplementation. *Acta Physiologica Scandinavica, 173,* 223-230.

Bjornebekk, A., Mathe, A. A., & Brene, S. (2005). The antidepressant effect of running is associated with increased hippocampal cell proliferation. *International Journal of Neuropsychopharmacology, 8,* 357-368.

Bourne, E. J., Brownstein, A., & Garano, L. (2004). *Natural relief for anxiety: Complementary strategies for easing fear, panic, and worry.* Oakland, CA: New Harbinger.

Bouton, M. E. (1993). Context, time, and memory retrieval in the interference paradigms of Pavlovian learning. *Psychological Bulletin, 114,* 80-99.

Bouton, M. E. (1994). Conditioning, remembering, and forgetting. *Journal of Experimental Psychology: Animal Behavior Processes, 20,* 219-231.

Bremner, J. D., Vythilingam, M., Vermetten, E., Adil, J., Khan, S., Nazeer, A., Afzal, N., McGlashan, T., Elzinga, B., Anderson, G. M., Heninger, G., Southwick, S. M., & Charney, D. S. (2003). Cortisol response to a cognitive stress challenge in posttraumatic stress disorder (PTSD) related to childhood abuse. *Psychoneuroendocrinology, 28,* 733-750.

Cahill, S. P., Franklin, M. E., & Feeny, N. C. (2006). Pathological anxiety: Where we are and where we need to go. In B. O. Rothbaum (ed.), *Pathological anxiety: Emotional processing in etiology and treatment* (pp. 245-265). New York: Guilford Press.

Cain, C.K., Blouin, A. M., & Barad, M. (2003). Temporally massed CS presentations generate more fear extinction than spaced presentations. *Journal of Experimental Psychology: Animal Behavior Processes, 29,* 323-333.

Cardoso, S. H. (2007). Hardwired for happiness. In C. A. Read (ed.), *Cerebrum 2007: Emerging Ideas in Brain Science,* pp. 169-184. Washington, DC: Dana Press.

Carey, P. D., Warwick, J., Niehaus, D. J. H., van der Linden, G., van Heerden, B. B., Harvey, B. H., Seedat, S., & Stein, D. J. (2004). Single photon emission computed tomography (SPECT) of anxiety disorders before and after treatment with citalopram. *BMC Psychiatry, 4,* 30-38.

Charney, D. S. & Drevets, W. C. (2002). Neurobiological basis of anxiety disorders. In K. L. Davis, D. S. Charney, J. T. Coyle, & C. Nemeroff (eds.), *Neuropsychopharmacology: The Fifth Generation of Progress.* Philadelphia: Lippincott, Williams & Wilkins.

Claparede, E. (1951). "Recognition and "Me-ness." In D. Rapaport (ed.), *Organization and pathology of thought.* New York: Columbia University Press.

Coplan, J. D., & Lydiard, R. (1998). Brain circuits in panic disorder. *Biological Psychiatry, 44,* 1264-1276.

Crocker, P. R., & Grozelle, C. (1991). Reducing induced state anxiety: Effects of acute aerobic exercise and autogenic relaxation. *Journal of Sports Medicine and Physical Fitness, 31,* 277-282.

Davis, M., Myers, K. M., Ressler, K. J., & Rothbaum, B. O. (2005). Facilitation of extinction of conditioned fear by D-cycloserine: Implications for Psychotherapy. *Current Directions in Psychological Science, 14,* 214-219.

Dishman, R. K. (1997). The norepinephrine hypothesis. In W. P. Morgan (ed.), *Physical Activity and Mental Health.* Philadelphia, PA: Taylor & Francis.

Dozois, D. J., Frewen, P. A., & Covin, R. (2006). Cognitive theories. In J. C. Thomas, D. L. Segal, & M. Hersen (eds.), *Comprehensive Handbook of Personality and Psychopathology, Vol. 1: Personality and Everyday Functioning,* pp. 173-191. Hoboken, NJ: Wiley.

Drosopoulos, S., Schulze, C., Fischer, S, & Born, J. (2007). Sleep's function in the spontaneous recovery and consolidation of memories. *Journal of Experimental Psychology: General, 136,* 169-183.

Eifert, G. H. & Heffner, M. (2003). The effects of acceptance versus control contexts on avoidance of panic-related symptoms. Journal of Behavior Therapy and Experimental Psychiatry, 34, 293-312.

Eisch, A. J., Cameron, H. A., Encinas, J. M., Meltzer, L. A., Ming, G.L. & Overstreet-Wediche, L. S. (2008). Adult neurogenesis, mental health, and mental illness: Hope or hype? *Journal of Neuroscience, 28,* 11785-11791.

Foa, E. B., Huppert, J. D., & Cahill, S. P. (2006). Emotional processing theory: An update. In B. O. Rothbaum, (ed.), *Pathological Anxiety: Emotional Processing in Etiology and Treatment.* New York, NY: Guilford Press.

Forbes, D., Creamer, M., Phelps, A., Bryant, R., McFarlane, A., Devilly, G. J., Matthews, L., Raphael, B., Doran, C., Merlin, T., & Newton, S. (2007). Australian guidelines for the treatment of adults with acute stress disorder and post-traumatic stress disorder. *Australian and New Zealand Journal of Psychiatry, 41,* 637-648.

Furmark, T., Tillfors, M., Mateinsdottir, I., Fishcher, H., Pissiota, A. Langstrom, B.,& Fredrikson, M. (2002). Common changes in cerebral blood flow in patients with social phobia treated with citalopram or cognitive-behavioral therapy. *Archives of General Psychiatry, 59,* 425-433.

Gigerenzer, G. (2004). Dread risk, September 11, and fatal traffic accidents. *Psychological Science, 15,* 286-287.

Guastella, A. J., Richardson, R., Lovibond, P. F., Rapee, R. M., Gaston, J. E., Mitchell, P., & Dadds, M. R. (2008). A randomized controlled trial of D-cycloserine enhancement of exposure of therapy for social anxiety disorder. *Biological Psychiatry, 63,* 544-549.

Hale, B. S., & Raglin, J. S. (2002). State anxiety responses to acute resistance training and step aerobic exercise across eight weeks of training. *Journal of Sports Medicine and Physical Fitness, 42*, 108-112.

Jacobson, E. (1938). *Progressive relaxation.* Chicago: University of Chicago Press.

Johnsgard, K. W. (2004). *Conquering Depression and Anxiety through Exercise.* Amherst, N.Y.: Prometheus Books.

Kilpatrick, D. G., Koenen, K. C., Ruggiero, K. J., Acierno, R., Galea, S., Resnick, H. S., Roitzsch, J., Boyle, J., & Gelernter, J. (2007). The serotonin transporter genotype and social support and moderation of posttraumatic stress disorder and depression in hurricane-exposed adults. *American Journal of Psychiatry, 164*, 1693-1699.

Kushner, M. G., Kim, S. W., Donahue, C., Thuras, P., Adson, D., Kotlyar, M., McCabe, J., Peterson, J., & Foa, E. B. (2007). D-cycloserine augmented exposure therapy for obsessive-compulsive disorder. *Biological Psychiatry, 62*, 835-838.

LeDoux, J. (1996). *The Emotional Brain: The Mysterious Underpinnings of Emotional Life.* New York. Simon & Schuster.

Leonard, B. E. (1997). Action mechanisms of antidepressants. In A. Honig & H. M. van Praag (eds.), *Depression: Neurobiological, Psychopathological, and Therapeutic Advances.* (pp.459-470). Hoboken, NJ: John Wiley & Sons.

Liang, K. C. (1999). Pre- or post-training injection of buspirone impaired retention in the inhibitory avoidance task: Involvement of amygdala 5-HT1A receptors. *European Journal of Neuroscience, 11,* 1491-1500.

Manji, H. K., Drevets, W. C., & Charney, D. S. (2001). The cellular neurobiology of depression. *Nature Medicine, 7,* 541-547.

McLean, P. D., & Woody, S. R. (2001). *Anxiety Disorders in Adults: An Evidence-Based Approach to Psychological Treatment.* New York: Oxford University Press.

Meredith, I. T., Friberg, P., Jennings, G.L., Dewar, E. M., Fazio, V. A., Lambert, G. W., & Esler, M. D. (1991). Exercise training lowers resting renal but not cardiac sympathetic activity in humans. *Hypertension, 18,* 121-130.

Milham, M. P., Nugent, A. C., Drevets, W. C., Dickstein, D. P., Leibenluft, E., Ernst, M., Charney, D., & Pine, D. S. (2005). Selective reduction in amygdala volume in pediatric anxiety disorders: A voxel-based morphometry investigation. *Biological Psychiatry, 57,* 961-966.

Mineka, S., & Zinbarg, R. (2006). A contemporary learning theory perspective on the etiology of anxiety disorders: It's not what you thought it was. *American Psychologist, 61,* 10-26.

National Institute for Health and Clinical Excellence. (2007). Anxiety (amended): Management of anxiety (panic disorder, with or without agoraphobia, and generalized anxiety disorder) in adults in primary, secondary and community care.

Neumeister, A., Bain, E., Nugent, A. C., Carson, R. E., Bonne, O., Luckenbaugh, D. A., Eckelman, W., Herscovitch, P., Charney, D. S., & Drevets, W. C. (2004). Reduced serotonin type 1-sub(A) receptor binding in panic disorder. *Journal of Neuroscience, 24,* 589-591.

Nielson, K. A. (1994). Beta-adrenergic receptor antagonist antihypertensive medications impair arousal-induced modulations of working memory in elderly humans. *Behavioral & Neural Biology, 62,* 190-200.

Otto, W., Pollack, M. H., & Sabatino, S. A. (1996). Maintenance of remission following cognitive behavior therapy for panic disorder: Possible deleterious effects of concurrent medication treatment. *Behavior Therapy, 27,* 473-482.

Petruzzello, S. J., & Landers, D. M. (1994). State anxiety reduction and exercise: Does hemispheric activation reflect such changes? *Medicine & Science in Sports & Exercise, 26,* 1028-1035.

Petruzzello, S. J., Landers, D. M., Hatfield, B. D., Kubitz, K. A., & Salazar, W. (1991). A meta-analysis on the anxiety-reducing effects of acute and chronic exercise: Outcomes and mechanisms. *Sports Medicine, 11,* 143-182.

Physicians' Desk Reference: PDR. (2004). Oradell, N.J.: Medical Economics.

Pitman, R. K., Sanders, K. M., Zusman, R. M., Healy, A. R., Cheema, F., Lasko, N. B., Cahill, L., & Orr, S. P. (2002). Pilot study of secondary prevention of posttraumatic stress disorder with propranolol. *Biological Psychiatry, 51,* 189-192.

Porto, P. R., Oliveira, L., Mari, J., Volchan, E., Figueira, I., & Ventura, P. (2009). Does cognitive behavioral therapy change the brain? A systematic review of neuroimaging in anxiety disorders. *Journal of Neuropsychiatry and Clinical Neurosciences, 21,* 114-125.

Salkovskis, P. M., Clark, D. M., Hackmann, A., Wells, A., & Gelder, M. G. (1999). An experimental investigation of the role of safety-seeking behaviours in the maintenance of panic disorder with agoraphobia. *Behavior Research & Therapy, 37,* 559-574.

Sapolsky, R. M. (1998*). Why Zebras Don't Get Ulcers: An Updated Guide to Stress, Stress-Related Diseases, and Coping.* New York: W. H. Freeman and Company.

Sing, C. F., Stengard, J. H., & Kardia, S. L. (2003). Genes, environment, and cardiovascular disease. *Arteriosclerosis, Thrombosis, and Vascular Biology, 23,* 1190-1196.

Sloan, T., & Telch, M. J. (2002). The effects of safety-seeking behavior and guided threat reappraisal on fear reduction during exposure: An experimental investigation. *Behaviour Research and Therapy, 40,* 235-251.

Stein, M. B., Kerridge, C., Dimsdale, J. E., & Hoyt, D. B. (2007). Pharmacotherapy to prevent PTSD: Results from a randomized controlled proof-of-concept trial in physically injured patients. *Journal of Traumatic Stress, 20,* 923-932.

Tada, K., Kasamo, K., Ueda, N., Suzuki, T., Kojima, T., & Ishakawa, K. (1999). Anxiolytic 5-hydroxy-tryptamine1A agonists suppress firing activity of dorsal hippocampus CA1 pyramidal neurons through a postsynaptic mechanism. *Journal of Pharmacology and Experimental Therapeutics, 288,* 843-848.

Tata, P. R., Rollings, J., Collins, M., Pickering, A., & Jacobson, R. R. (1994). Lack of cognitive recovery following withdrawal from long-term benzodiazepine use. *Psychological Medicine, 24,* 203-213.

Thoren, P., Floras, J. S., Hoffmann, P. & Seals, D. R. (1990). Endorphins and exercise: Physiological mechanisms and clinical implications. *Medicine & Science in Sports & Exercise, 22,* 417-428.

Thwaites, R., & Freeston, M. H. (2005). Safety-seeking behaviours: Fact or function? How can we clinically differentiate between safety behaviours and adaptive coping strategies across anxiety disorders? *Behavioural and Cognitive Psychotherapy, 33,* 177-188.

Vaiva, G., Ducrocq, F., Jezequel, K., Averland, B., Lestavel, P., Brunet, A., & Marmar, C. R. (2003). Immediate treatment with propranolol decreases posttraumatic stress disorder two month after trauma. *Biological Psychiatry, 54,* 947-949.

Walsh, R. & Shapiro, L. (2006). The meeting of meditative disciplines and Western psychology: A mutually enriching dialogue. *American Psychologist, 61,* 227-239.

Wells, A., Clark, D. M., Salkovskis, P. M., Ludgate, J., Hackmann, A., & Gelder, M.G. (1995). Social phobia:

The role of in-situation safety behaviours in maintaining anxiety and negative beliefs. *Behavior Therapy, 26*, 153-161.

Westra, H. A., Stewart, S. H., & Conrad, B. E. (2002). Naturalistic manner of benzodiazepine use and cognitive behavioral therapy outcome in panic disorder with agoraphobia. *Journal of Anxiety Disorders, 16*, 233-246.

Westra, H. A., Stewart, S. H., Teehan, M., Johl, K., Dozios, D. J., & Hill, T. (2004). Benzodiazepine use associated with decreased memory for psycho-educational material in Cognitive Behavioral Therapy for panic disorder. *Cognitive Therapy and Research, 28*, 193-208.

Wilkinson, P. O. & Goodyer, I. M. (2008). The effects of cognitive-behaviour therapy on mood-related ruminative response style in depressed adolescents. *Child and Adolescent Psychiatry and Mental Health, 2*, 3-13.

Wolitzky-Taylor, K. B., Horowitz, J. D., Powers, M. B., & Telch, M. J. (2008). Psychological approaches in the treatment of specific phobias: A meta-analysis. *Clinical Psychology Review, 28*, 1021-1037.

You, S., Gujar, N., Hu, P., Jolesz, F. A., & Walker, M.P. (2007). The human emotional brain without sleep—a prefrontal amygdala disconnect. *Current Biology, 17*, 877-878.

Topic Index

This index is intended to help you to locate specific information regarding key terms, concepts and images.

About the Authors

Catherine M. Pittman, Ph.D., HSPP

Catherine has a B.S. from Central Michigan University, as well as a M.S. and Ph.D. in Clinical Psychology from Northern Illinois University. She is an Associate Professor at Saint Mary's College in Notre Dame, Indiana. As a licensed clinical psychologist with Memorial Hospital and in private practice in South Bend, Indiana, she has specialized in the treatment of brain injuries and anxiety disorders.

Elizabeth M. Karle, MLIS

Elizabeth has a history of panic disorder with agoraphobia. She has a Bachelor's degree from the University of Notre Dame, a paralegal certificate from Roosevelt University in Chicago, IL, and a Master's in Library and Information Science from Dominican University. Elizabeth is the Collection Management Supervisor at the Cushwa-Leighton Library at Saint Mary's College in Notre Dame, Indiana. She is the author of *Hosting a Library Mystery: A Programming Guide*.

LaVergne, TN USA
17 March 2011
220542LV00001B/142/P

9 780615 309040